Thanks for all the years of loyalty

11/11/21

OVERCOOKED

Ivan Sayles

with
Paul Goldstein

AS IS
BOOKS

OVERCOOKED

Copyright© 2021 by Ivan Sayles
All rights reserved. No part of this publication may be translated, reproduced, stored in a retrieval system or transmitted, in any form or by any means, electronic, mechanical, photocopying, recording or otherwise, without express written permission from the author.

Published by **AS IS Books**, an imprint of:

Peter Weisz Publishing, LLC
7143 Winding Bay Lane
West Palm Beach, FL 33412 USA
peter@peterweisz.com

Sayles, Ivan • All rights reserved
        Exposé—Memoir — Biography — Self-Help — Entertainment

ISBN: 9 781667-112015

Printed in the United States of America by Blurb.com
1 2 3 4 5 6 7 8 9 10

Page layouts and cover design by Peter Weisz Publishing, LLC, West Palm Beach, FL
www.peterweiszpublishing.com

Dedication

I would like to honor two extraordinary lives, cut short by the devastating disease of addiction. David Sattanino and Veronica Birk were two of my employees and friends who didn't live to see past their 26th birthdays. They were two special souls who passed away within a year of each other, taking with them two heartwarming laughs we'll never hear again, two beautiful faces and their smiles we'll never see again. They were loved by their families and stolen from us at an early age by drugs; two people who influenced me in life, and inspired me in their deaths. The loss of these souls has helped me persevere to finish my book, and through my writing their lives will continue to have purpose in helping others understand what it is like to be an addict.

I hope this book will inspire you and give you insight into the affliction that contributed to Dave's, Veronica's, and thousands of other untimely deaths. I hope reading this will cause you to take action, as America continues its feeble attempts at defense against the pandemic known as addiction.

OVERCOOKED

In Memoriam

Manuel Señorans Dominguez
September 14, 1963 - April 21, 2021
Brother, husband, father, grandfather.
CHEF

Manuel was my dear friend and college roommate at the Culinary Institute of America. Taken from us far too soon due to the pandemic that has left no family untouched.

—*Ivan*

OVERCOOKED

Contents

Author's Prologue v
Introduction. 1
Chapter One: You Can Smoke Crack etc. 3
Chapter Two: The Smithville Café, 1982 9
Chapter Three: My Addiction 13
Chapter Four: Polar Bear Swim 19
Chapter Five: Where Is Cory's Finger? 27
Chapter Six: Crack Whores 31
Chapter Seven: Jones Beach and My First Love 37
Chapter Eight: Fun at the Beach 45
Chapter Nine: The Chapter Without a Name 51
Chapter Ten: In the Beginning 55
Chapter Eleven: Lock and Load 61
Chapter Twelve: Arrest Number Two 67
Chapter Thirteen: Three Mistakes I Made 71
Chapter Fourteen: March 13, 2004 – Amanda 83
Chapter Fifteen: Busboys 93
Chapter Sixteen: Arrest Number Three 97
Chapter Seventeen: I ♥ NY 99
Chapter Eighteen: My First Christmas 103
Chapter Nineteen: Recovery 107
Chapter Twenty: Jail 113

Photo Section 125
Chapter Twenty-one: What a Cloud Smells Like 141
Chapter Twenty-two: Maggots 153
Chapter Twenty-three: How to Become a Crack Addict 159
Chapter Twenty-four: Captain Ivan and 1st Officer Eddie 165
Chapter Twenty-five: It's Way Too Expensive 169
Chapter Twenty-six: Hold On, I'll Get You a Glass 175
Chapter Twenty-seven: Arrest Number Four 183
Chapter Twenty-eight: The Little Blue Pill 189
Chapter Twenty-nine: Sometimes You Have to Drop Back 195
Chapter Thirty: The Stewards 205
Chapter Thirty-one: My Addiction II 213
Chapter Thirty-two: Rules & Regulations 219
Chapter Thirty-three: My Near-Gay Experience 225
Chapter Thirty-four: I Must Have Fallen Asleep 229
Chapter Thirty-five: Really Good Bad Luck 235
Chapter Thirty-six: CPCS 7 239
Chapter Thirty-seven: Me, Jen & Gov. Andrew Cuomo 245
Chapter Thirty-eight: My Three Moms & Paul Goldstein .249
Acknowledgements 256

Author's Prologue

If ye then, being evil, know how to give good gifts unto your children, how much more shall your Father who is in heaven give good things to them who ask him?
—Matthew 7:11

Flying home with Amanda, June 2017

Your small body is curled up in the seat next to me—eyelids closed tight, sealing in all your hopes and dreams, protecting you from the future that's just over the horizon. I look at you, tracking the rhythm of your every breath as we sail through the sky at light's speed. Your eyes moving back and forth under your lids, I wonder how my 13-year-old daughter sees me in her dreams. As you lie beside me, I stare at you, terrified of the way you'll see me when you grow older. You're still blissfully blind to my shortcomings, holding on to the pure unconditional love you have for your father. I see it in your eyes when you look up at me. But soon you'll come to realize just how human I really am. You'll discover my faults, realize my mistakes and failures, and learn of my addiction and the years it stole from us. Then I pray, oh God, I pray that you don't repeat my mistakes. But this is your life, not mine. You'll grow through adolescence into adulthood and make your own way. Sweetheart, I want all your dreams to come true. As I look at your small body gently rising and falling with every breath, I don't think I've ever loved you more than I do at this moment in time.

OVERCOOKED

Introduction

I've been thinking about writing for some time, dabbling with a paragraph or story here and there, but it wasn't until 2018 that I made the commitment to put my life into words. This is where I begin…first, distancing myself from an ugly past by casting off and setting sail on my personal voyage of atonement, freeing the demons that have been trapped inside me since birth. I make my reparations with a keyboard, embarking on this journey not only as therapy for myself but also in the hope of giving insight to those who to read it.

This is for parents, friends and relatives of addicts who ask, why is my child doing this? Why has my loved one abandoned us? Why does everything I try to do drive them further and further away? I'll give you my personal perspective into the way an addict thinks and feels. It may prove to be graphic and repulsive at times, but try your best not to judge. That is not for us to do; instead we must be compassionate, offer guidance and most importantly, understand.

I believe there are three important things to remember when dealing with addiction, especially if it's your friend or loved one.

1. No matter how powerful you think you may be, you're powerless against the disease of addiction.
2. Addicts themselves are the only ones who possess the cure for their affliction.

3. They did not plan this, nor did they do it to hurt you. If you're asking yourself, "How could they do this to me?" Put this book down. You're not ready to read it

—Ivan Sayles

June, 2021

Chapter One

You Can Smoke Crack and Fuck Other Women, Or You Can Have Everything Else in the World

After spending the latter half of the summer of 2009 as a guest at the Nassau County Correctional Center in East Meadow, Long Island, I was released in early September and cannot begin to describe how wonderful it felt to breathe the warm summer air of freedom. The first thing I did upon my release from jail was exactly what I was instructed to do: go straight to the Nassau County Probation Office to meet my probation officer.

When I checked in, the gentleman at the front desk pulled my file and told me that my probation officer was out in the field. The gentleman told me not to worry, that he would let my officer know I had checked in. Later that afternoon, I discovered my probation officer had left me a nasty voicemail, threatening me with arrest because I failed to go straight from jail to see him. And so began my wonderful three-year relationship with The Nassau County Probation Department.

The second thing I did was what I'd been dreaming about while sitting in my cold, dank cell that summer: I took my turn-of-the-century 34-foot Sea Ray with twin gas-burning 454s out for a cruise. Well, to be accurate, the cruise was the third thing I did. The second was taking one of the longest, hottest showers of my life. It was all I could do to scrub the stench of jail off my body, a stench that seeped under my skin like a tattoo. It's not that I had spent a long time incarcerated or suffered some terrible fate like being raped in the shower. I did, however, spend enough time behind bars to understand that I needed to make a profound change in my life.

Living and working near the ocean and having owned a boat for most of my adult life, there is no better therapy for my soul than a solo cruise out on the open water. Boarding the "Amanda Hope" that warm September day was like reuniting with an old friend. I practically tore the green canvas from its snaps as I popped them open one by one, uncovering her shiny laminated deck. The keys were right where I had left them, in the ignition. I pumped the throttle levers back and forth several times, priming her engines, held the shift levers at half-throttle and turned each of her two keys. Just as ordered, her two engines responded, roaring to life, emitting a bluish white cloud of burnt oil and exhaust fumes that only come from a gasoline engine that has been sitting dormant for a time.

The gentle westerly breeze knew exactly where my nostrils were, sending the cloud right into my face. Normally, I would have held my breath as the acrid smoke flowed past me at the helm and out into the open water, but not today. Today, I savored the aroma as if waving a fine cigar under my nose in anticipation of its pleasure. As the boat warmed up, I untied her lines and cast off, beginning the ride through the twisting canal that leads from my house to the open water. Hampered by the damned 5 mph speed limit enforced on residential waterways, it made the 15-minute ride to open water seem like an hour.

I needed to be on the water. I needed to think. I needed to clear my head. As I passed Cap's, a waterfront eatery I frequented by boat and by car, I waved to Amy, the owner, who was chatting with customers on the deck. Despite this being a simple everyday experience, a chill ran up my spine with the realization that if my life did not do a total about-face immediately, I could very well end up spending the next part of it caged up like an animal instead of enjoying warm summer days like this one.

I headed south out of Seamans Creek, I increased my speed gently as I swung westward toward Goose Creek. Her engines were now thirsty for fuel so I eased forward on the levers. She was teasing me as her bow started to rise ever so slightly. We leveled off for a few seconds, then I slammed her throttles forward. Her engines roared in response, guzzling fuel at the rate of 24 gallons per hour. She lurched forward like a whale breaching the surface, and I gently eased back on the gas.

We planed off and settled down to a comfortable cruising speed. I prepared myself for an easterly turn into Bulkhead Drain, approaching the sparsely marked entrance into this navigable but hazardous channel that leads out to the Great South Bay. I had seen many a pleasure craft run aground at the mouth of the channel and I was not about to allow the "Amanda Hope" to be one of them. Once I was safely in the channel, I settled into my groove and lit a cigar—an Acid Blondie Belicoso, since you were about to ask. I was now at peace…at peace within myself.

Gliding along the sea with the front half of the boat completely out of the water, I could hear and feel the whoosh of the water as it passed under the hull, occasionally tossing a drop or two over the gunnel and onto my face. The water is like glass today, I thought to myself. There was not another boat in sight or a cloud in the sky. I glanced back and saw small twin rooster tails of water spitting up from the propellers. The trail of my wake marked my path for as far back as I could see. I savored the warm moist summer air blowing across my face. This is my own private heaven, I thought. I'm untouchable here, all alone on the water with only God and Mother Nature to share it with.

The one thing you do plenty of in jail is think, and I thought a lot about how and why I had come to be where I was. All I could think about as I glided along the bay, greedily soaking up more than my fair share of the remaining bliss of summer, was a visit from my girlfriend on one of my last days locked up. She gave me an ultimatum. Her words were barely above a whisper and I leaned across the visitors table so I could hear. They say if you want to be heard, speak softly: it forces the person you're talking to concentrate and listen. What she said caused the tiny light bulb in my head to spark, and it illuminated my soul. She said, "You can smoke crack and fuck other women, or you can have everything else in the world."

You see, for the two years prior to that statement, I'd been smoking crack cocaine just about every day and not giving a rat's ass about anything or anyone else in the world besides myself. I hadn't cared about my friends, my family, my business or even my 4-year-old daughter, Amanda. All I thought about was getting high.

In the beginning, I had it all. I thought I was fooling everyone, but it was only me I was fooling. I was getting high and convinced myself I was functioning normally in society. Maybe I pulled it off for the first few months, but probably not. I was living out my fantasies in my own private drug-induced reality. Nights were about the thrill of getting high, and by day I played the part of the secret agent, living the "normal" life.

It was a game to me, one that has been played by thousands of people before I ever came to the table, by people far smarter and wiser than I. It's a game that takes on all comers; everyone is welcome at its table. It's clear to me now that I want no part of it. It's way too expensive, and the stakes are much too high.

There is no doubt it's being played right now: maybe someone just moments ago has won the game. Oh Lord, I hope not. I don't know why I thought I was special or why any addict thinks they can beat the game. We all think that way. We think we can beat the odds…or more accurately, that the odds don't exist for us. It's such a thrill, rolling the dice with every hit, every pull on that glass pipe rising higher and higher and closer to the win. I never won. Thank God, for the only prize in the game of addiction is death, and when you've reached its highest level, there is no replay.

It may seem so simple to give up two little things, smoking crack and fucking other women, in exchange for everything else life has to offer. To simplify it even more, it's actually only one thing, because giving up smoking crack in crack houses undoubtedly leads to not fucking crack whores. A no brainer, right? Her words were barely above a whisper and I leaned in close so I could understand. Give up one thing and I can have everything else in the world. Everything! If I just give up that one little thing?

On paper, yes, it seems so simple, but in a mind infected by addiction, it is not. In order to have "everything else," I would have to get an evil little monkey off my back. I had smoked away nearly $200,000.00 in cash and gotten arrested five times within a year and a half before finally landing behind bars. Over a two-year period my addiction alienated me from all my friends and relatives, drove five properties into foreclosure, and put my restaurant in danger of being padlocked for back taxes.

As I'm about to turn 54, I can't help but realize just how lucky I am. My life is an open book *(I couldn't resist that)*. As I share my story with people I will never meet, it is my therapy and also your warning. As an alcoholic would stand up in front of a room of strangers and tell his story, I will tell you mine. I write for the sake of Dave and Veronica and the thousands of others who can no longer speak for themselves, to try to give you an understanding of the disease from the perspective of an addict. I'll tell you the funny, the sad, the pathetic and the perverse. I write for myself just as much as I write for you. I'm a lucky man, one of a small percentage to survive a disease that for most users ends in either jail or death. The disease of addiction is as devastating and undiscriminating as cancer, with a relapse rate that's through the roof. "Hi, my name is Ivan, and I'm a drug addict."

OVERCOOKED

Chapter Two

The Smithville Café, 1982

he Smithville Café was a restaurant built in the 1800s in my hometown of Bellmore, on Long Island. Bellmore used to be called Smithville, until for some reason the Long Island Railroad decided to name the train stop in the town of Smithville the "Bellmore Train Station," thus changing the name of the town from Smithville to Bellmore. I attended Wellington C. Mepham High School, which gained nationwide infamy when some dumb kids on its football team decided to stick pine cones up the asses of other kids on the same football team. Google that one, if you like.

I first started cooking during my sophomore year of high school, tinkering around in the kitchen at home. At my father's suggestion, I went to BOCES for culinary arts. The Board of Cooperative Educational Services offered a half-day vocational school that served multiple districts in Nassau County. BOCES taught courses like cosmetology, culinary arts, carpentry, auto body work, and veterinary science. A bus drove around to the schools in my district to pick us up after lunch and haul us to BOCES, which turned out to be the perfect opportunity to goof off, smoke pot, and get into all sorts of mischief in between classes.

OVERCOOKED

One young entrepreneurial veterinary science student used to steal the chloroform they used to euthanize the rats in the lab. If you're not familiar with chloroform, you are probably familiar with a scene from any scary movie when the bad guy puts a rag over the hero's mouth and the hero gets knocked out. That's chloroform. This entrepreneurial student would repack it in 2-ounce vials and sell them on the bus for two bucks each. We would dab a paper towel in the chloroform and hold it under our noses to inhale its sweetness. It wasn't enough to knock us out, but just enough to make our bus ride that much more enjoyable.

My second-year instructor, Bill Montarulli, was a graduate of The Culinary Institute of America in Hyde Park, NY, and was the main reason for my continuing my education beyond high school. In my senior year, we took a class field trip to the CIA. After our tour, we had lunch and I applied to college. I had no prior restaurant experience, and since that was a requirement to get admitted to the CIA, I had to do something quick. I applied for a job at a local restaurant, situated between my high school and my house, called the Smithville Café. In the early '80s, big chain restaurants had not yet grabbed a foothold on Long Island. Applebee's, Chili's, and the like, were still years away, so it was the local mom-and-pop restaurants people still frequented.

The Smithville was the only local place I knew of that had a decent reputation. I walked in the door, found the chef, Ronnie, and asked for a job. To my disappointment, he told me they weren't hiring. I tried explaining that I had applied to culinary school and desperately needed work experience, but he wasn't budging. Finally, I offered to work for free a few hours a day after school, to get the experience I needed to get into culinary school. The chef was no fool; he knew a good deal when he saw one. We shook hands and at 16 years old I was in the restaurant business.

This was not my first job, nor my first shrewd business negotiation. At 13 I had gotten a job at a clothing store owned by my uncle Sol and his son Eric. For two dollars an hour, I unpacked boxes, stocked shelves and put price tags on clothes. I counted the days until my 14th birthday when I would be of legal age to get my working papers. When my birthday arrived, I pulled my uncle aside and informed him I was now of legal working age and demanded he increase my pay to the legal minimum wage of $2.35 an hour. He agreed, and two years later I quit my paying job at Jax and Jeans to work for free at the Smithville Café. Shrewd!

I did prep work during the week after school, and on weekends I worked the pantry station, eventually carving a niche for myself and wiggling my way onto the books for some pay. I graduated high school and went on to start culinary school that December. I would drive home on weekends and bus tables at the Smithville Café.

With cash in hand, and the drinking age at 18, I began going out to bars and drinking after work. There, I met other people in the restaurant and bar business doing the same thing I was: drinking after work 'til the wee hours. Those fine people introduced me to another friend, cocaine. This turned into an expensive habit, until I discovered I could buy coke on Long Island and sell it to my friends in college. Ugh!

OVERCOOKED

Chapter Three

My Addiction

I am a drug addict and will be for the rest of my life. The choice to stay clean is mine, and mine alone. I have a disease that unless you have it yourself, is quite difficult to fully understand. Addiction affects the young and the old, the rich and the poor. It is a parasite that drains the life from its host, by stealing the very essence of his or her humanity. Each addiction is as unique as the user it consumes. Yet, it has a cure, and it is by far the simplest, least expensive cure of any ailment in the world: Don't do drugs!

Unfortunately, that's much easier said than done. The odds of beating a crack cocaine habit are less than the odds of beating cancer. Statistically fewer than 5 percent of crack addicts who enter rehab are successful in beating their addiction. Rehab centers are a good step toward sobriety if the addict is ready to get clean; they are a waste of time, money and resources if he or she is not.

There is a reason rehab centers don't promote their success rates. It wouldn't be great marketing for a TV commercial to depict a serene scene on the beach with a massage table and sunset in the backdrop while boasting a 95 percent failure rate, right? Rehab is not the cure-all, so don't be fooled by the fancy ads and empty promises by healthy-looking sales reps who claim they are recovered addicts. Twenty-eight days does not cure an addict. Twenty-eight days in rehab will sober up an addict, for sure, but until the addict is ready to be cured, a program is useless. If and when an addict is ready for treatment, however, a rehab center is a great place to start. Too many people think rehab is the cure-all for addiction, like taking seven days of antibiotics, so it doesn't sting when you pee anymore. Take your heads out of the fucking sand people; addiction is a serious killer disease.

Although I've been drug-free for years now, I can't say using doesn't enter my mind every now and again…but not in the sense that I have an urge to light up a stem and take a hit. No, it's far more deceptive than that. It's not like confronting my enemy on an open battlefield. My demons are well-trained insurgents that could teach ISIS a thing or two. They creep up on me; a memory of a situation or a feeling that reminds me about something I did, felt or saw when I was getting high. I get these weird feelings deep inside me, the "heebie jeebies," I've come to call them. It's like a chill amassing at the base of my spine and creeping upward, vertebra by vertebra. This chill, I've come to realize, is the frigid breath of the demon that lives within me, lying in wait for me to weaken so that he may awaken. As time goes by, it happens less and less. I never know what may trigger it: a smell, a place, something someone says…I never know, but boom! It's there in an instant. It's so hard to describe. It's not an urge to get high, per se. It's more of a back-door approach, like the thought of getting high or the memory of the feeling of being high, but not the actual urge to use again. More like my body is remembering the sensations of the drug, the euphoria, the hunger for it, but then I'm suddenly repulsed by it.

I simultaneously fear, yet yearn for that sensation, while reminiscing about a time that once was. Perhaps it's akin to throwing the winning touchdown pass at the big game in high school. Relishing in the thrill of that moment that you can never have again, because it was only a reality for a split second, yet your mind wants to relive it over and over. Then, bang! Suddenly my brain gets word of what's going on throughout the rest of my body and tells everyone to calm the fuck down; it ain't happening. Poof! The thought is gone. What's for lunch?

What needs to change is the way people think about the cure for addicts. The general consensus is black and white: you're an addict or you're not, either you're using or you're clean. On paper that's entirely correct, but add in the human factor and it's so much more complicated. It's about things you can't see or touch. What force on earth could take an honest, hardworking person, from a good, loving home, who cares for his family, and metamorphose him into a thieving, lying, self-serving parasite?

The answer is the all-consuming, powerful force of addiction. Be it drugs, alcohol, gambling or sex, every addict has within himself or herself a personal demon lying in wait, ready to strike at the slightest weakness. My drug of choice (or DOC, as they call it in the biz) is cocaine, specifically crack cocaine. It's not for me to understand why I'm addicted to cocaine. If you told me I would end up dead or in jail if I ever smoked a cigarette, shot heroin or took a sip of orange juice ever again, I would steer clear of those things just as easily as I would skirt around a puddle on the sidewalk. But tell me I can never use cocaine or I would end up dead or in jail, and my mind starts spinning.

There are plenty of people who use cocaine and don't have a problem. It's a recreational drug, right? Maybe I could just use it on weekends and be okay? Maybe only on my birthday or while I'm on vacation? No, no, and no, I can't! Not now, not ever. No addict can ever touch his or her DOC again if he wants to live a normal life. You can lock us up, send us to AA or put us into rehab over and over, but until we make the decision for ourselves to make a change, none of it will help. We'll be back on the shit in no time.

It took me over a year and a half from the time I decided to get clean until I was actually able to stay straight. My first serious attempt to get clean was in April of 2008 after my first arrest. That night, my friend and I picked up two girls and brought them back to a hotel to get high, which at that point, was pretty much what my entire life consisted of. Get some shit, grab a girl, and hide from the world. The partying would go on for three or four days straight. Then I would pass out, wake up and start all over again.

As my friend and I were getting into our second night of doing nothing but smoking crack and getting our dicks sucked, the inevitable happened: we ran out of shit. The last thing any male drug addict wants is a crack whore needing another hit in the middle of his blowjob. Now, I don't mean the term 'crack whore' in a pretentious or demeaning way. Seeing as I was one of the four crack whores in the room, I feel I've earned the right to use that phrase as I please.

Anyway, with dick sucking no longer an option and my having very little patience even when I'm not strung out on drugs, I went on a run to pick up more crack. The smart thing to do, if there was a smart thing to do in this case, would have been to call someone to deliver. But why would I do the smart thing? I borrowed my friend's car instead of taking my restaurant's catering van, which I had been driving temporarily. This saved the company van from being impounded that night, but in the end was just a temporary reprieve for the doomed vehicle. Several months later I wrecked the van, slamming into two parked cars after falling asleep at the wheel because I'd been up for days smoking crack. I was driving the catering van since I had flipped my brand new Volvo with less than 1,500 miles on it after falling asleep at the wheel because I was up for days smoking crack. Do you see a pattern here? I didn't.

I had wrecked three cars and each time walked away unscathed. I got pulled over numerous times with drugs on me, and up to that point had escaped arrest. Every time I got away with something, it made me feel more invincible, making me even more brazen in my activities. Taking a hit of crack on the Southern State Parkway while cruising at 70 miles an hour was as common to me as listening to music while driving.

Think about that next time you're on the road with your kids and see if that doesn't piss you off. But, that's who I had become.

That's who every addict becomes. Addiction eats you up from within, to the point that getting high and your selfishness are the only things that matter. The disease has a unique way of producing a blinding insanity that causes the addict to take the path of self-destruction that no sane person would ever take.

Anyway, by the time I met the dealer, I was getting pretty strung out. It had been about 45 minutes since my last hit and I was starting to crash hard. He hopped in my car and we made the exchange. No sooner than he'd closed the door, I was lighting up, pulling as hard as I could on the glass pipe, waiting to exhale and feel the sensation of the drug flowing through my veins. Now that I was high again, I was getting anxious to get back to the hotel room.

I must have been driving quite erratically before I got pulled over. As the police officer approached the car, I rolled down my window. I'm sure I looked every bit the part of the strung-out druggie who had been up smoking crack for days. The officer started questioning me about where I had been and where I was going. I told him that my friend and I had switched cars and that I was on my way to the hotel to meet him and get the work van back. This seemed like a plausible story to me at the time, but in sober retrospect, it likely didn't take the officer two seconds to figure out what I was up to at 3 a.m. on a weeknight.

He went back to his car to run my license. When he came back, he told me my license was suspended and asked me to step out of the car. He then told me I was going to be arrested for aggravated unlicensed driving, handcuffed me and put me in the back of the patrol car. By this time, a second officer arrived and together they began to search the car, which is when the real fun began.

In New York State, aggravated unlicensed driving means that your license has been suspended, and you've been notified of the suspension but you continued to drive. In my case, the suspension was for failing to pay tickets, as I was too busy smoking crack to be bothered with paying them. Criminal possession of a controlled substance aside, Nassau County Police take driving with a suspended license very seriously, since there have been numerous instances of people driving under the influence, like myself, while their license was suspended, like myself, and getting in accidents and killing people, unlike myself, thank God.

Their search of the car amassed 3.5 grams of crack cocaine, which is just enough coke to make it a B felony possession charge, punishable by a minimum of one year in prison. The New York State Liquor Authority also frowns on letting people have liquor licenses with drug felonies, so I had that going for me, too, as a restaurant owner.

I also had two scales and a couple of crack pipes. The cops wrapped up my arrest nicely by topping it all off with a DUI charge. This arrest, being my first of five over the next year, landed me in jail and subsequently on probation for three years. At my sentencing, the Judge took my license away for three years. That sentence was given along with the statement that if I was caught driving without a license again, he would put me back in jail. That threat and my wonderful experience during my "short stay" at the Nassau County Jail became a strong enough deterrent to keep me off the road when I got out of jail.

After getting bailed out from that arrest in April 2008, almost a year and a half before serving my sentence and ultimately getting clean, I enthusiastically began an outpatient program at South Oaks Hospital in Massapequa, NY. I had had enough. That was it! I was turning my life around; I was getting the help I needed from the right people. I changed my cell phone number and deleted my contact list. I took the necessary precautions to erase the connections I had to my dealers and fellow crack addicts. I swore I was getting my life back on track. But it didn't take. Within a month, I was off to the races again, smoking the glass pipe, falling back into the darkness of my addiction and right into the arms of the police. This time it was a precinct in Queens, my second arrest for criminal possession of a controlled substance.

Chapter Four

Polar Bear Swim

I have many fond memories of my days at the Culinary Institute of America. Like most things in life, you get out of it what you put into it. I treated culinary school about as nonchalantly as I treated high school: as a big party. I'm no celebrity chef with my own cooking show, but I know my way around a kitchen. Culinary school gave me the tools to run a successful restaurant, a crash course in every aspect of the food service business.

My college education was divided into three trimesters consisting of hands-on experience, classroom education and externship. The curriculum has changed drastically since I graduated, and now offers both associate and bachelor's degrees in culinary arts or baking. In my days at CIA, they offered a two-year associate degree, comprising 7- or 14-day crash courses in every aspect of the restaurant business: accounting, wines, legal, baking, ordering and receiving, butchering, and more. They even had a culinary French class, which didn't do me much good, as even today, every time I write, "Passed hors d'oeuvres" on a catering contract, I have to ask Siri how to spell it. Talk to my editor, Heidi, about my spelling. Bon appétit!

I'm extremely proud of the fact that today I participate in the Culinary Institute of America's Externship program, helping train future chefs and restaurateurs. The externship program is a six-month, hands-on work-in-the-field program at the halfway point of a degree. Dave Sattanino, to whom this book is dedicated, did his externship with us and then returned after graduation as a manager at two of our restaurants, Rachel's and NAWLINS, as well as two of our catering halls.

We didn't even have a business for him to work in when Dave started his externship at Rachel's, because the restaurant had been destroyed by Superstorm Sandy. I think Dave's first job with us was hauling construction debris out to the dumpster, which he did with the same smile and enthusiasm as everything else in his life. My partner Rich and I took advantage of the devastation by doing a complete reconstruction of the building, including a redesign of the kitchen.

Dave was invaluable during construction and with the grand reopening of Rachel's in the spring of 2013. He was serving as an assistant manager that summer before returning to school with one of the best hands-on experiences any student could have: the construction and opening of a restaurant. After graduation, he returned to become our catering manager at the Nassau County Bar Association and Freeport Yacht Club. When it was time to construct and open NAWLINS, there was Dave, building and managing his second restaurant by the age of 24. What a bright future he had. He had dreamed of becoming a sommelier and had begun studying for it, but on January 9, 2017, that dream died, along with Dave, from an opioid overdose.

One thing I've always taken seriously is working hard to make money. During my time at CIA, I had a few jobs that included butchering deer during hunting season for 25 bucks a carcass (pun intended), working on a garbage truck, and cooking at a German restaurant near school, The Old Heidelberg, as well as driving home on weekends to work at the Smithville Café. With the exception of the Smithville, I worked all of these ventures with two classmates of mine, Chris and Cory. I met Chris at the Boardwalk Restaurant during my externship, and Cory was Chris's friend. Chris was a short, stocky guy from Long Island who came from an old-school Italian family and used pronunciation like bad-troom instead of bathroom and olive earl instead of olive oil. I can remember many a Saturday night, going out drinking after working at the Boardwalk Restaurant, then dropping Chris off at home at five in the morning...and his grandmother was already up making sauce in the kitchen for Sunday night dinner.

Cory was from Upstate New York, a few towns away from CIA. He was a 6' 2", 225-pound African American who should have been a linebacker, not a chef. It was Cory's father who owned the sanitation company we used to collect garbage for a couple of days a week. Chris and I got up at 4:30 in the morning with Cory, who would drive the truck with Chris and me hanging off the back, picking up the pails. Residential garbage pick-up in Poughkeepsie was done privately, not by the municipality, with several sanitation companies competing for the business. That made our route extremely inconsistent, as houses on the same block were serviced by different companies. Our route would take us all through the scenic mountains and towns along the Hudson River—beautiful in the spring, nice in the summer, breathtaking in the fall but absolutely brutal in the winter.

Well, one man's garbage is another man's gold. Needless to say, our dorm room soon became the collection point for anything in decent shape that other people didn't want: pots, pans, hot plates, furniture, and massive amounts of pornographic magazines, all of which were not allowed in the dorms. Not that dorm rules were very important to us; at one point I even had my dog, Lambchop, living with us.

We lived in C dorm, one of three two-story dormitories on campus surrounding a pond affectionately named Lake Veloute, after one of the five mother sauces. The back of B and C dorms overlooked the Hudson River and in fall and winter, the view from the back of the dorms was postcard-worthy.

In the fall, foliage in shades of browns and oranges cascaded down the mountainside to the river, water glistening as it flowed south to Manhattan and out into the Atlantic. In winter, the slope of the mountain on the other side of the water was covered in snow, with huge chunks of ice floating downriver, was equally spectacular. On the east bank of the river, diesel trains ran along the old Hudson River Line with commuter and freight cars traveling north and south from Grand Central Station in Manhattan to Albany and beyond.

Our dorm room consisted of three twin beds—two of which could be stacked into bunk beds—three desks, three chairs and a bathroom with a shower. Two illegals resided in our dorm room: Corey, who was asked to live off campus after his first trimester, slept in a sleeping bag on the floor, and Lambchop, my future ex-fiancée Mary's dog. She named him Lambchop because she thought it was cute with my being in culinary school and all. He was a mischievous 40-pound mixed breed with one nut. We called him Uno.

Uno's last day at Culinary Institute started at 4:30 a.m., when my alarm went off. I was taking a class called "Pantry," and had to be dressed, in class, and ready to cook by 5 a.m. Pantry should have been called "Brunch," because that's what it was. We cooked breakfast for the students and staff. With the exception of when you're the students doing the cooking,"Pantry" is one of the perks of being a culinary student. Let me tell you, we didn't slap together bacon, egg, and cheese sandwiches for breakfast: the plates we were putting out could have been served at The Plaza.

I lumbered out of bed in the dark, walking barefoot on the worn carpet, trying not to disturb anyone. I tip-toed over Cory, who was snoring in his sleeping bag and as my right foot came to the ground, I felt something warm and mushy squishing between my toes. It was the unmistakable sensation of stepping barefoot into fresh, warm dogshit. I lost it; I grabbed Uno by his neck, and rubbed his nose in his feces while scolding him. I know better than that now, don't worry. As he cowered away, he headed for the safety of Cory's sleeping bag for some emotional support. Just as I turned the shower on to rinse off my foot, I heard Cory screaming bloody murder as Uno was licking Cory's face.

Well, needless to say, everyone was up. I got dressed, threw on a coat and went outside to take Uno for a walk. It was a bitter-cold, 20-degree February morning. The sun wasn't going to rise for another hour or so, and most of the light was coming from the snow blanketing the campus. I didn't bother with the leash. Uno was usually good about not straying off, but that morning I guess he knew I was pissed, and he darted right out onto the frozen Lake Veloute, which was completely frozen over but for the northeastern side where a stream fed the pond.

As Uno was sniffing around on the lake looking for a good place to take a piss, he headed closer and closer to the northeast corner. I scooted down the 10-foot ravine onto the ice, calling for him to come to me. This led him farther and farther away until, splash! he fell through the ice. Uno was frantically clawing with his front paws, yipping and whining while desperately trying to get up on the ice. But there was no way in hell he was going to do it by himself. So, out onto the lake I went.

Uno had fallen through the ice about 15 yards from the shore. As I approached him, I threw off my gloves and lay down on the ice, spreading my legs and arms out in an effort to distribute my weight evenly. I slithered on the frozen lake, inching closer to the dog, the thinning ice creaking and moaning beneath me. I was stretching every tendon and muscle, trying to reach him. Just as I managed to get a finger in his collar and pull him toward me, the ice gave way.

I was scared but I didn't panic. I realized very quickly that despite all my winter clothing, I was still able to tread water. My adrenaline was pumping hard. Aside from the initial shock of the freezing water when I fell in, I was pretty surprised that I didn't feel cold. I didn't feel anything, really. I got my shit together quickly, grabbed Uno with both of my arms, one hand around the collar and the other on his tail. With a spinning move, I slid him up on the ice. Man's best friend took off like a rocket toward the shore and left me behind like a bad habit, treading in cold, black water.

Now that my first priority, of getting the dog out, was taken care of, I began feeling the chill of the water. I was looking around, trying to figure out my next move, when I saw in front of me a student standing on the shore holding a branch in one hand and extending his hand out to me with the other, which was an extremely nice gesture and would have worked great, had his arms or the stick been 50 feet longer, but at this point he was as useless to me as Uno's one nut was to him.

I was flailing my arms from above my head down to my waist, in a sort of butterfly-stroke move, trying to get my body on top of the ice to climb out, but every time I put my weight on the ice with my chest, it just kept crumbling beneath me. All the while, I was staring straight at this idiot on the shore. I finally said to him, "You can walk out at least 40 feet before this ice gets thin. What good are you doing over there?" He said nothing; he just continued to stare at me, holding the branch with one hand and waving at me to come toward with the other. Boy was this guy inspiring.

I continued my icebreaking breast stroke until I got to some solid ice, positioned myself parallel to the break in the ice, put my face down in the water and just rolled over onto my back, up on the solid surface. Getting out of the frozen pond ended up being a lot easier than I expected. I doubt I was in the water more than two or three minutes, but it definitely felt like a lot longer. I stood up dripping wet, walking toward the guy on the shore who was staring at me with a puzzled look. I didn't say a word to him. He started to ask me what I was doing in the water, and I just shook my head as I walked by, giving him one of those 'tell it to the hand' waves.

I can honestly say, I have never been so cold in my life. Uno was rummaging around the grass by the lake and it took me a few more minutes to grab him. When we got back to the room, I had to pound on the door because my fingers were so cold I couldn't get my key in the lock. Cory opened the door, gave me a look and said, "What the fuck?" I walked right past him to the bathroom, stripped down and got into the shower, running cold water on the dog and me, gradually raising the temperature over the next few minutes.

Since Uno and I had caused quite a ruckus that morning, I thought it might be a good idea for him to move in with my parents until Mary and I got engaged and moved to Massachusetts. Apparently, word spread fast that morning, because when I got to class, everyone was talking about *the guy who went for a swim in Lake Veloute*.

OVERCOOKED

Chapter Five

Where Is Cory's Finger?

While Chris and I did our externships at Jones Beach, Cory went to butcher school in Chicago. Cory got his restaurant experience, to meet his prerequisite to gain entrance to CIA, at The Old Heidelberg in Dutchess County. The chef and owner was Dieter Kuller, a German immigrant whose father had been a butcher in the old country. He had a thick accent and was every bit the stereotypical German. His restaurant was immaculate and super-organized, and he was stubborn and vulgar as hell. Dieter was known to have stuck his finger between one of the waitresses's legs, put it to his nose and asked, "Karla, when are you going to wash that thing?"

In addition to working the garbage route, Cory got Chris and me jobs with him at the Old Heidelberg. Everything we made there was from scratch. Twice a week, Dieter would purchase whole sides of veal and butcher them. We made Sauerbraten, Wiener schnitzel, goulash, and rouladen from that meat. We froze the legs until we had enough shanks to run an Osso Buco special and made demi-glace from the rest of the bones. Nothing was wasted.

It was Dieter who taught us to butcher venison during hunting season. Once we were trained, Dieter let us use the back of the restaurant to butcher deer the hunters brought in and even let us keep the $25 fee. Dieter's share of the deal was one cut of meat per deer, which he put in the freezer. Then when hunting season was over, he would host a free venison dinner for all of his customers.

He pulled out all the stops, making chops, Sauerbraten, goulash, sausage and even salami from the venison. Diners paid for their booze and Dieter fed them for free. He threw a pretty nice shindig and his customers really loved it.

After Cory's return from his butcher school in Chicago, he thought he was a kind of a big deal and began bragging about how good he was. Dieter was having no part of Cory's bravado—not in his house! So he decided to put an end to it. One day, Cory, Chris and I were summoned to the prep room, where there hung two sides of veal. Dieter said to Cory, "You think you're such a big deal? Let's see." Dieter challenged him to see who could break down a side of veal faster and directed Chris and me to our seats, where we were to judge the contest.

Cory went into his bag and got a couple of his shiny new knives and a leather holster he obtained from butcher school. Wagers placed, they put their aprons on, ran their blades over their steels and stood poised, knives in hand, in front of their respective slabs of meat, waiting for the countdown. Dieter gripped his aging grey carbon steel Dexter boning knife so hard his knuckles were white, while Cory, standing at his side, held a shiny new stainless Henckel with a sharpening steel holstered on his belt. No way Dieter was going to let anyone beat him at his own game in his own house. Right then and there Chris and I should have called no contest.

Like two gunslingers in the middle of town waiting for the clock-tower bell to strike, they stood waiting to draw down on each other. "Ready…Set…Go!" Knives flashing, pieces of fat were flying off the carcasses. Dieter began taunting Cory, while calmly slicing the animal in fluid movements like an artist painting a canvas. As they progressed, Cory got nervous, sweat beads forming on his brow; he slashed in quick jerky motions. There was much more than money hanging on this contest: there was pride.

It was clear to us in the first few minutes who would win. They were both going at a pretty good pace as Dieter continued to taunt Cory. "You piece of shit, you call yourself a butcher? You couldn't cut an apple in half." "What did they teach you in that worthless butcher school?" The beads of sweat began dripping down Cory's face. He was beginning to waver and then suddenly let out a bone-chilling scream. He had sliced off the end of his finger. This didn't faze Dieter one bit as he continued to butcher his side of veal, still taunting Cory—who was starting to turn white and was bouncing around in a panic, holding his bleeding finger with a rag, pleading, "My finger, my finger! Where's my finger?"

Dieter, in all of his glory, also started jumping around the room, like a heavyweight champion after knocking out his opponent, flexing his muscles and screaming, "You bastard. You think you're better than me? You fuck with me and I'll kill you!" Chris and I were now trading off between calming Cory down and holding back Dieter, all the while looking for the tip of Cory's finger, which we couldn't find right away because it was stuck on the top of Cory's shoe.

OVERCOOKED

Chapter Six

Crack Whores

There is a standing joke among druggies: What's the difference between a crack whore and a person who smokes crack? A person who smokes crack will help you find your missing wallet. A crack whore will steal your wallet and then try to help you find it. The thing is, when you are addicted to drugs, you don't think like a rational person. In your mind, you do. You think you're in control, but if you could step back and look at yourself from the outside, it would be clear that you're not rational.

When you're under the influence, you're convinced it's everyone else who's nuts. You know better than everyone, and no one can tell you what to do. It was in this disillusioned bubble that I lived every day of my life for two years. This is the world of addiction. It's a filthy place with dirty, selfish people, lying, stealing and using each other with one goal in common: to get high. I had become just as much a crack whore as any of the people I speak about.

There are several ways to smoke crack cocaine. The easiest, most popular (and my preferred method), is to roll up some screens, stuff them into the end of a glass tube called a pipe or "stem" and pack them down with a "pusher." A pusher is any object skinny enough to fit into the glass. A round metal object like a pin from a door hinge works best; so does a chopstick, as long as you don't mind smoking a few bamboo flecks.

OVERCOOKED

There aren't too many stores out there that specialize in the sale of glass crack pipes, but rest assured there are plenty of gas stations, smoke shops and convenience stores that sell little flowers in glass tubes. It may surprise you that buying a crack pipe on Long Island is about as easy as buying a lottery ticket.

They are sold everywhere—not just in shitty neighborhoods—but in the stores you frequent within a mile of your own house. If you live in Nassau or Suffolk counties, I guarantee you've seen them behind the counter of your local gas station or convenience store. They even sell them at the gas station 150 yards east of the Nassau County Police 7th Precinct in my hometown of Seaford, NY.

Next time you buy a lottery ticket, pack of cigarettes or soda, or you pay for a fill-up, take a look behind the attendant. If you see a black box behind a checkout counter that says pipe screens on it, you've hit the jackpot. They come in gold and silver and sell for about a buck a package. Once you've found the screens, I'll bet my bottom dollar the glass pipes are there, too.

Most of the time, the pipes are hidden under the register or blocked from view. Since they can't be sold as crack pipes, they come with tiny artificial flowers inside them—a miniature version of a single-stem rose wrapped in clear plastic you see in 7/11s and supermarkets. If you've got some balls, ask the attendant for a pack of screens and a glass and see what happens. The pipe should set you back another buck or two and after that, all you'll need is a lighter. For a grand total of about four bucks, you're all set to go hit up your dealer for a nice crack rock.

Before I learned how to make crack from powdered cocaine, I used to drive the streets of Hempstead looking for crack. The best way for me to get it was not from a dealer on the street. Heck, I was a white boy driving around the ghetto in a brand new $50,000 Volvo, too easy a mark for the streetwise dealer and his buddies. No, the best way to cop some shit was to find another addict who knew the streets, knew the dealers and had the same primal cravings as I did.

Who could I find to help me make the transaction? A crack whore, that's who. Sure, I would get ripped off here and there, especially in the beginning when I first met a girl. But once I established a rapport with her, she realized she was far better off hanging out with me for a few days, shacked up, partying in a hotel room, than stealing 50 bucks from me and calling it a day. In a short time I had developed several of these mutually beneficial situations.

Once the purchase was made, it was time to smoke. We couldn't go back to my house, at least not early on in my addiction when I used to try to separate my real life from my surreal life, so we would go to a hotel. No, not the kind with a concierge and room service: I would choose a seedy joint where management looks the other way at prostitution and drug dealing, the kind of disgusting place where you can bribe the clerk into booking you into a used room for around 20 bucks. In case you're unfamiliar with the term "used room," it's just as gross as it sounds. It's a room that has been used for a short stay; the guests have left but the maid hasn't cleaned it yet. The clerk at the desk re-rents the room "as is." He pockets the money without the owner knowing, and you get the filthy room. It's a win-win for both parties.

I frequented several of these places. I had no preferences. I would go with anyone who could help me get crack: black, white, old, young. It did not matter. We would get high for days on end, maybe having a slice of pizza or a hamburger between drug runs. We'd fuck, living in filth with the fleas and the bedbugs, smoke crack and fuck some more. I can't ever remember taking a shower during these binges, because that would mean taking my eyes off of my money, keys and more importantly, my drugs—and I had learned that lesson the hard way.

I was hanging out with a skank on the fourth floor of a sleazy hotel in Hempstead called The Courtesy. We'll call her the white girl, for the purpose of this story. We'd been smoking and fooling around for the better part of the night, but she was on and off her cell phone constantly, which was starting to annoy me. When I asked her what was up with that, she told me she had a friend who wanted to get high, too, and that her friend would fuck me if I gave her a hit of crack.

Well, that sounded like a good deal to me, so I told her to invite the friend up. She was a cute, young, black girl, maybe 5' 3" with a hot little body. She wasted no time grabbing the crack pipe and mounting me, as I lay naked on the bed. She slid up and down on me while I took a hit and drifted off in euphoria. That warm feeling of being inside a woman combined with the feeling of ecstasy from taking a hit had become my Achilles' heel.

These girls were pros and knew exactly how to work me. When I came down from my hit and looked around the room, I noticed the white girl was gone. I threw the black chick off of me and ran into the bathroom looking for her, but she wasn't there. The whole thing was a freakin' set-up. While I was in la-la land getting high and fucking the black girl, the white chick had gone into my pants pockets, grabbed my keys and was headed down to my car to steal the rest of my stash.

I got dressed and bolted out of the room and down the stairs, praying she had not stolen my car. The black girl must have called her on her cell phone because she was nowhere to be found in the parking lot. I ran back up the stairs to the room and poof! There they both were, acting like nothing had happened. They told me she had just gone down to grab a cigarette from my car, which was a lie. She gave me back my keys and I went down to the car to check my stash, and it was gone. I didn't even bother going back up to the room. I was certain they were gone, too. I just drove home.

As time went by, I became more entrenched in the drug life and the way things worked. My crack-smoking friends and I had developed a circle of crack whores we used to hang around with. As I look back on the way we treated those women, I can't help but feel disgusted with myself. I never did anything to physically hurt anyone, but the values normal people place on other human beings had all but evaporated for me. I can remember how funny I thought it was at the time when I was with two of my crack-smoking buddies, thinking about which girls to call.

One of the guys, Tony, asked Mark if he could get a particular girl's phone number. Mark, being very protective of his little harem, didn't want to give Tony the number. Tony asked if Mark was planning on seeing her that night and Mark said no. Tony's response was, "Well, if you're not using it tonight, why can't I?"

This comment from Tony elicited side splitting laughter out of Mark and me, a laughter I can still hear ringing in my head when I think back to that time. Except now it rings with disgust and degradation—a symbol of just how low my thoughts of a fellow human being had become.

OVERCOOKED

Chapter Seven

Jones Beach and My First Love

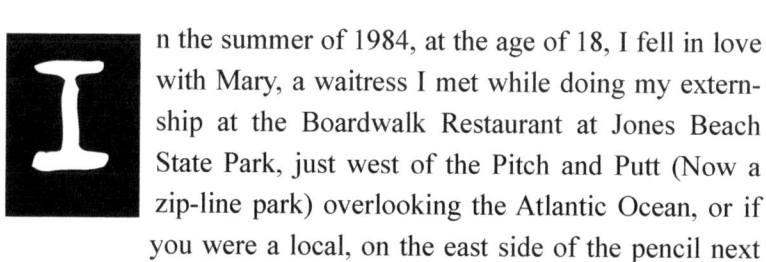

In the summer of 1984, at the age of 18, I fell in love with Mary, a waitress I met while doing my externship at the Boardwalk Restaurant at Jones Beach State Park, just west of the Pitch and Putt (Now a zip-line park) overlooking the Atlantic Ocean, or if you were a local, on the east side of the pencil next to the par 3. This was to be my first of two failed nuptial plans with waitresses from that restaurant.

The Boardwalk was a 450-seat behemoth of a restaurant/catering hall with three dining rooms located right on the Boardwalk overlooking the Atlantic Ocean, hence the witty name. It was a big rectangular building with floor-to-ceiling windows on the south, east and west sides, and outdoor dining terraces on the east and west sides, adding an additional 150 seats for fair-weather dining.

The terrace was a favorite station of the waitstaff because of the high customer traffic and low managerial supervision. Hell, why would managers leave the confines of a nice air-conditioned space if they didn't have to? This left a certain freedom for the service staff on the terrace that was not available at the inside dining rooms to, let's say, consume beverages that were ordered "by mistake" from the bar, disappear with friends while another server covered their station for 1/2 hour, or smoke cigarettes... things of that nature.

OVERCOOKED

One waiter in particular who managed to finagle many of his shifts outside was nicknamed Terrace Tom. The biggest thing going for Terrace Tom one summer was when Darryl Strawberry came in for lunch. We had a Reuben sandwich on the lunch menu, a classic NY deli sandwich made of corned beef or pastrami (the fattier the better, in my opinion), sauerkraut, Swiss cheese and a schmear of Russian dressing on rye, and then grilled. Perfect! But Mr. Strawberry knew better and ordered two pastrami and American cheese sandwiches on white bread, to the horror of the entire kitchen staff and anyone who has ever set foot in a genuine New York Kosher-style deli. He washed them down with four Scotches, followed by a cigarette. Then he was off to Shea Stadium to play a night game—the pride of the NY Mets, their 1st round draft pick in 1980.

The north third of the Boardwalk building and entire basement were the 'back of the house.' Downstairs we had men's and women's locker rooms and showers, a loading dock, dry storage, a liquor room and walk-in refrigerators and freezers. We had separate refrigerators for meats, produce, fish, dairy and so forth.

Donald Trump, a mere real estate developer at the time, but very well known in NY, along with Marla Maples, graced us with his presence for dinner one evening on his way to a show at the Jones Beach Theater. He left a very nice tip for the server as I recall. Then later, around the year 2000, he attempted to rebuild the restaurant but was stymied because NY State supposedly would not allow him to build a basement in the new building. That's all I'll say about that. You can research it if you want. President Trump has enough people talking about him these days and doesn't need my two cents.

I ended up spending a good part of my youth at the Boardwalk through the ages of 18 to 27, leaving for a time then coming back and rising to the position of head chef at both the Boardwalk and Captree Cove Restaurant at Robert Moses State Park. It would become a major influence in my life, teaching me much about the logistics of running restaurants, on- and off-premises catering, as well as introducing me to my lifelong friend and business partner Rich and best friend Eddie.

I worked long hours with the same group of people, then we'd go out drinking and sniffing coke, well some of us sniffed coke but we all drank 'til the wee hours. Grab a few hours' sleep and start all over the next day. Several of us developed a special bond that still exists today. I might not see my friends for months, but when we do get together it's like we saw each other yesterday, which is a great barometer of true friendship.

In those days, the drinking age was 18, and my rookie season at the beach consisted of working all day, drinking and sniffing coke all night and driving everywhere. Blessed by youth, I felt invincible. I could do anything. We worked 80-hour weeks in the kitchen, and the waiters and waitresses often worked six doubles in a row.

We had it down to a science: working anything over 80 hours a week resulted in taxes that reduced our overtime rate to less than $4.00 per hour, so it wasn't worth working over 80 hours. When we did, we made arrangements to get those hours transferred to the following week. If you're wondering what we got paid back then, I'll save you the math: minimum wage was $3.35 an hour in 1984. If a Local 3 guy in Manhattan worked 80 hours at today's rates, with overtime and double-time on Sundays, he'd be grossing around $6,000 for the week. We took home around $360. Boy, we showed them, didn't we?

Forty years ago, driving-while-intoxicated laws were on the books but not enforced like they are now. It wasn't uncommon to be pulled over by a cop and either driven home or told to lock up your car and walk home, where your car keys would be waiting for you in your mailbox. After a while, enough drunken kids like me, driving around without our seatbelts, because wearing them did not become a law in NY until 1984, either got killed or killed enough innocent people to piss off enough moms to get MADD enough to pressure our police to enforce our DWI laws. Thank you for that, MADD!

Anyway, back to the end of the '84 season: Mary returned to college at Oneonta and I finished my externship and went back to CIA, driving back and forth to see her on weekends. No sooner than I graduated, I proposed to Mary. I was a 21-year-old line cook, and all I had to my name was my job and a Buccaneer Red, 1973 Olds Omega with a white vinyl top and rocket 350. God, I loved that car. I had no money, but with 50 bucks down and 40 bucks a month for I can't remember how long, I bought an engagement ring from Zales. With that done, when Mary graduated, we decided to move to Boston, where I got a job at the oldest restaurant in Boston right next to Faneuil Hall.

I remember telling my father I was engaged and moving to Massachusetts. We were standing on the front steps of the house and he looked at me with surprise. I watched as his eyes welled up with tears, thinking then that they were tears of happiness. I know better now. I was barely 21 and he was certain I was making a mistake.

I was strong-willed and determined; it would have been futile for him to try to talk me out of it and he knew it, so he did the only thing he could. He hugged me, wiped his eyes and wished me luck. What a horrible feeling it must be to be a parent watching your child do something you know is a mistake and not being able to do anything about it. My father did nothing—not from weakness, but from the incredible strength it takes to comprehend that your child is no longer under your control, and despite loving him more than anything else in the world, you must release him to find his own way.

Mary and I rented an apartment outside of Boston. She got a job managing a shoe store and I was hired as a fry cook at the oldest restaurant in Boston, the Union Oyster House. I loved it and quickly moved up to the sauté station, where I was one of five line cooks and was responsible for banging out 175 dinners by myself on a busy night. I was young, dumb and in love. Mary worked during the day from 10 a.m. to 6 p.m. and I worked nights from 3 p.m. to 11 p.m., and as we settled into our new lives, we saw less and less of each other. As time went on, I began banging a waitress and Mary began banging her regional manager. Needless to say, our relationship ended.

I had moved away from home to get married and was determined not to return with my tail between my legs. Spring was coming: time for a new beginning. I was recently single and sleeping on a friend's couch, when I found a job running the kitchen at a small restaurant in Chatham called The Sea in the Rough. It included room and board with the promise of a nice bonus at the end of the summer, so off to Cape Cod I went!

Come Labor Day, the season ended. The summer had gone well—at least I thought it had. The bonus never materialized, and when I brought it up, the owner claimed to have never said anything about a bonus. I should have quit on the spot, but like an idiot, I stayed on. I had become friends with the staff, especially the manager, Dave, and his wife Tammy. Plus, with the season over and things calmed down, I began to really enjoy living in Cape Cod.

I found out from Dave that this was not the first time the owner had promised a bonus and welched on it. I also found out the owner had promised that when he retired in a few years, he would sell Dave the restaurant. I kept in contact with Dave for a while after I left The Sea in the Rough, but I've long since lost touch with him and his wife. I hope he was able to purchase The Sea in the Rough from that prick.

With the restaurant open through December, I had no plans to leave, despite the bonus issue. But as fall approached, the owner and I started butting heads. I was just too dumb to read the writing on the wall. The season was over and there was no need for me or my salary anymore. It was October of 1986 and time for me and New England to part company. I'd had some good times and met some great people but it was time to go back home to Long Island.

I moved back just in time to watch Mookie Wilson's ball roll between Bill Buckner's legs, inspiring the Mets to go on to game seven and win the 1986 World Series. I moved back into my parents' house and they welcomed me with open arms. I quickly got a job as a sous chef with a large off-premise catering outfit called Stone Caterers, but that only lasted about three months. There was the right way, the wrong way, and the Stone Caterers' way. They did things just a little differently than everyone else. To this day it kills me that their Chicken Francaise was made with brown sauce and mushrooms as opposed to the lemon and wine sauce everyone else serves.

They also had a crew of old ladies (is that politically incorrect, or can we still say that?) making appetizers, which is fine if you're going to make fancy gourmet hors d'oeuvres. But no, they had the Golden Girls making mini knishes and pigs-in-a-blanket. Being a CIA graduate and my culinary prowess notwithstanding, it seemed to me that a machine could wrap a piece of puff pastry around a miniature hot dog or some mashed potatoes just as well as an old woman could.

I think the real reason for my grievance over this operation was that I really didn't want to be there at 6 o'clock in the morning to supervise. I was low man on the totem pole, so I guess when the new guy came aboard this would be his job. But until then I was intermittently wrapping up mini hot dogs, putting them in the freezer, and falling asleep in my coffee.

My final weekend there began with a wedding on a Friday night that got me home around 2:30 a.m. and I was back at the shop at 7:00 a.m. to do a deadly double. I packed up a truck with food and equipment for an afternoon anniversary party, drove to the location, set up, served, cleaned up, packed up and drove back to the shop. After we unpacked, I grabbed a fresh crew, loaded the truck and started all over again for a wedding that evening. By the time we got back to the shop, unpacked and locked up, it was 6 a.m. I was exhausted.

I went home for a shower and a nap. The next morning, after working a 23-hour day, I showed up to work at 9 a.m., one hour late. I was immediately summoned into the manager's office for a tongue-lashing on punctuality. I couldn't believe it! I had just worked a 23-hour day, gotten two hours' sleep and was back on the job. I stared at him with my jaw hanging open. I was speechless. When he was done, I simply did an about face, and as George Thorogood said, "Out the door I went."

OVERCOOKED

Chapter Eight

Fun at the Beach

In the summer of 1984, I was home from college and scheduled to start my externship the following week. Hoping to relax a few days between college and work, I made plans with my friends to go to Jones Beach and enjoy a day by the water. Since I made my externship arrangements over the phone and hadn't met the chef, I figured as long as I was at the beach I'd stop in and say hello before I started working the following week.

I walked in donning my swim trunks and a T-shirt, found my way into the kitchen and introduced myself to the chef, Eric Bunch. He shook my hand, gave me a quick tour of the place, and showed me where the uniforms and locker rooms were. I'm not exactly sure how it happened, but the next thing I knew, I was dressed in whites and an apron, standing in front of a huge two-compartment sink filled with eight bushels of little-neck clams waiting to be shucked and turned into baked clams.

I hadn't shucked a dozen clams in my entire life before that day. I shucked for almost five hours, opening more than 3,000 clams. My pruned left hand had turned a pinkish-white color and looked like it had gone through a cheese grater, taking nick after nick from broken clam shells. The fat fleshy part of my palm below the pinky was slashed and bleeding from where the clam knife slipped and slashed my skin countless times. When I was finished, I went back to see the chef. As he began to explain my next assignment, I told him I wasn't supposed to start work until the following week and that my friends were waiting on the beach for me. He said he understood, no problem. "Be here tomorrow at 8 a.m. for brunch." Ugh.

Volume Services leased the Boardwalk Restaurant from New York State, making us accountable to two sets of bosses: our corporate bosses and our State bosses. The title of the local big cheese for the State, Mike A., was...ready for this? Deputy Regional Director of the New York State Office of Parks, Recreation, and Historic Preservation. Mike saw himself as more of a restaurateur than a Deputy Regional Director of the New York State Office of Parks, Recreation, and Historic Preservation.

He was a common sight at the restaurant and micromanaged it as if it were his own. He personally dictated many of its menu items and the design of the menu itself. He made sure we served his favorite things, down to his favorite drink: raspberry iced tea. Two of his daughters were waitresses there, and it was not unheard of for someone he didn't like to lose his or her job. In my 19-year-old opinion, he spent way too much energy on one restaurant for someone who was supposed to be running all the State Parks on Long Island.

It turns out that Mr. A. was a much bigger deal with the State than I would have guessed, based on his title. I found this out one night when another cook named Steve Ducey, Mike A.'s younger daughter Tracy, her friend Danielle (both waitresses) and I went out on my boat. It was a 21-foot single-screw Bayliner, probably not newer than 1972. Mike's older daughter, Ellen, was dating Steve's older brother, Eric, who was a student in Nevada at UNLV. This fact about Eric may seem irrelevant at the moment, but it will come into play later.

We headed out in the early evening to Club California, a waterfront club in Island Park. Steve and I heard if we wore our boxer shorts that night, we got a free drink, so we did. I have to say, Steve and I were a bit set back when the bouncer at the door told us the boxer short deal was only for women and we were the only two idiots that showed up in boxer shorts that evening. We were more upset about not getting the free drink than being the only two guys in boxer shorts at the club.

We met several other people from the beach and danced, drank, and laughed 'til 3:00 in the morning, when the four of us decided to head back home. BWI, or Boating While Intoxicated, is a big offense nowadays, but 30 years ago no one gave a shit if someone drove their boat drunk, least of all me, or anyone I was with that night.

So, we cast off without a care in the world, without a spotlight, at low tide, on a dark, moonless night. I navigated my way through the canals and out into the State Channel, otherwise known as Reynolds Channel, a straight body of water running east-west, that separates the mainland from the barrier beaches and runs between the Rockaway inlet otherwise known as Debbs inlet and the Jones (Beach) inlet, then all the way out to Fire Island.

As we turned east on the windless summer night into the wider water of the State Channel, we separated into couples: Danielle and I were in the driver's seat and Steve and Tracy were on the bench at the stern. I gave the boat some gas and she planed off. It was like driving on black glass, with the warm summer air blowing on us—silent except for the hum of the engine and the steady whooshing sound of the boat slicing through the motionless water.

I couldn't help but ease forward on the throttle a bit as the boat glided effortlessly through the night. The channel is pretty much a straight run. The key words here are pretty much. There is a marsh just east of the third hole at the Lido Beach Golf Course that extends north into the channel by about 60 yards and at low tide, it stands about 4 feet out of the water. In my case, this was about 10 yards too far and 4 feet too high. I hit the marsh on a pitch black night at 3/4 throttle, sending the 21-foot boat and its occupants flying into the air and landing about 20 feet up on the marsh.

It's a miracle none of us was hurt. We were banged up, bruised, and shocked for sure, but that was about it. It was pitch black and none of us had any idea where we were. Back in those days, only rich people had cell phones, so all we could do was wait until daylight, get our bearings and try to get help. As the sun came up, I realized we were on the marsh adjacent to the golf course. Steve had to report to work at 10 a.m. that day so he volunteered to leave, find a payphone, and call the girls' parents to let them know we were all OK. Then he'd call Seatow, which is like AAA on the water, so we could get towed off the marsh.

I bravely volunteered to stay behind with the women. Steve got to the main road, made all of his phone calls, then jogged the 8 miles from Lido to Jones Beach, and amazingly got to work on time. About two hours later, Seatow showed up. For $210.00 they attached a line from their boat to the bow hook of my boat, pulled the line taught then gave it some gas and spun my boat around and dragged her off the marsh and into the water, which was now only about 10 feet away, as the tide had risen. The whole process took 10 minutes. She was undamaged, save for some bottom paint scraped off during our slide, and she started right up. We continued our journey home, no worse for our ordeal, but with a great story.

Unbeknownst to us, at some point in the early morning all sorts of efforts had been launched to find Mike A.'s missing daughter. As everyone knows from watching cop shows, you can't file a missing person's report for 48 hours. Well, who knows if that's really true? But what I do know is that Mike A. sent NY State Troopers to my apartment, my parents' house and Steve and Eric's father's house at 6 a.m. to see if they knew where Tracy was. The Las Vegas police even paid her boyfriend, Eric, a visit to inquire as to her whereabouts. The helicopter search that began for Mike A.'s daughter at first light was called off as soon as Steve got to the road and found a payphone.

When Steve got to work, he found out the severity of what had happened and who the troopers had visited that night. He called his father to let him know everything was OK. Not knowing my parents' number and having no way to get in touch with us, he could not call them. The three of us had no idea what was going on until later that afternoon. Despite Mike's daughter being safe and sound, no one bothered to send the state troopers back to my house to tell my parents I was OK. Thanks for that one, Mike! You could send state troopers to my parents' house at 6 in the morning to tell them I was lost at sea, but couldn't be bothered to call them to tell them I was all right. Fuck you!

I suppose I should have just been thankful I didn't get fired.

OVERCOOKED

Chapter Nine

The Chapter Without a Name

In the spring I got a call from the chef of the Boardwalk Restaurant. We talked for a few minutes and I was offered the sous chef job. Externship aside, I began my official career at Volume Services, a food service giant, with stadium and college campus contracts all over the country. Locally, Volume Services had the food-service contract for Yankee Stadium, Jones Beach, Robert Moses and Captree State Parks, which included all the concession stands, an ice cream parlor, a pool, the 8,200-seat outdoor theater at Jones Beach and the 450-seat Boardwalk Restaurant.

After my two years as the sous chef of the Boardwalk, the chef became manager and I moved up the ladder to become chef, eventually running two restaurants for Volume Services: The Boardwalk Restaurant at Jones Beach and the Captree Cove Restaurant at Captree State Park. By 1991, I'd had my fill of the restaurant business and moved into restaurant supply, trying my hand as a foodservice salesman at J. Kings located in Oakdale.

I developed restaurant accounts from Manhattan to western Suffolk County, including my favorite territory of Fire Island. It's hard for a day of work to suck when it starts off by putting on a pair of shorts and sneakers then taking the ferry out of Bayshore across the Great South Bay. I would disembark at the ferry terminal in Ocean Beach and walk from one town to the next along Fire Island National Seashore. If the towns were too far apart or I had too much to schlep, I'd hop in a water taxi.

I didn't have to wear a jacket and tie: the dress was casual, and so were the attitudes of my customers. My time as a salesman afforded me the pleasure of driving all over the Island and getting a feel for different neighborhoods. It was during that phase of my life that I developed an interest in real estate. It was the early '90s and the country was in bad financial shape. We were in a recession, the savings and loan crisis of the late '80s into the mid-'90s ended and the real estate market had tanked.

In my spare time I started investing in real property on Long Island with my friend Vic. The majority of homes we bought were bank owned, fixer-uppers. We flipped most of them but ended up keeping some as rentals. After a few years of lucky investments, I had made a few dollars and quit my job as a salesman to seek my fortune in real estate.

For the better part of two years, I bought and sold single-family homes and I was now ready to up the ante and buy an apartment building. It was during my negotiating the purchase of a four-story apartment building in Lawrence, NY, that I stumbled on an ad for a waterfront restaurant in the business opportunity section of Newsday, and the rest, as they say, is history.

The Texas Ranger was a family-owned waterfront restaurant whose claim to fame was a 2 ounce hamburger that sold for 99 cents, known as the Special Burger (or as locals called it, the Ranger Burger). The restaurant was located in a strip on the south shore of Long Island known as the Nautical Mile, famous for its working waterfront community and restaurants, a destination that's been attracting tourists and locals for almost 100 years.

That restaurant would become Rachel's Waterside Grill…and my life for the next 24+ years. I built it up from nothing, with hard work and determination. She stood faithfully by my side as my life crumbled around me. I can honestly say she was my second love. I came within inches of losing her because of my addiction to crack cocaine. It then took years to build back up and pay off the hundreds of thousands of dollars of debt she went into in my absence. I'm thankful and proud of my partner and employees (some of whom are still with me today) who stood by Rachel's in her dark times. Together we have built a great restaurant, rising up to be voted Best Seafood Restaurant on Long Island four years in a row in 2011, 2012, 2013 and 2014 by Best of Long Island.

Ah, but nothing comes easy, and before I could accomplish that, I had to get the cocaine out of the way. Today I couldn't be prouder of my staff, who will prepare and proudly serve you a meal that is second to none! Rich or I might even dazzle you by sautéing a lobster dinner, making fresh mozzarella or a Caesar salad tableside and chatting with you for a while.

OVERCOOKED

Chapter Ten

In the Beginning

One of the problems with the public's perception of addiction is that they have been deceived into thinking the cure for addiction is rehab. Additionally, too many addicts go to rehab for the wrong reasons, because of pressure from their jobs or family, which ends in relapse rather than recovery. Many addicts, as well as friends, family and co-workers of addicts, are deceived into thinking that just by checking into a rehab center for 28 days, they'll walk out clean. Which they will—so where's the deception?

The overwhelming majority will pick up and use again. Showing up at the door of a rehab center and expecting a cure (like taking antibiotics for an infection) is a farce, and it only serves to fill the coffers of the companies that own the rehabilitation centers.

Sobriety means a total commitment and change in life. There is only one reason for an addict to go to rehab: the addict himself wants to be cured and wants it so bad that he's willing to make a lifelong commitment to sobriety and permanently change everything about his life. It is then and only then that he can be cured. Rehab is an excellent catalyst for recovery, but the true cure remains within the addict himself. There is only one way to achieve absolute sobriety: DON'T EVER USE AGAIN! Done!

It took me two years to accomplish never again, and never again is only as of right now. No one will ever know if it's never again for me until I'm dead and gone. I've seen people sober for 20 years who fall off the wagon. There is no rhyme or reason for this. I'm going on 11 years without sniffing coke or smoking crack. I have not feared using for quite some time, which is good and bad. Good because I got the monkey off my back, and bad because fear of using was what kept my guard up, preventing the evil from coming back into my life.

In the beginning, it was the fear of using that kept me clean. I was terrified of running into an old friend in the bathroom who would offer me a "bump" while I was under the influence of a few drinks. In the early months of my sobriety, the only time I would think about coke was when I peed. It might sound funny, but it had as much to do with surroundings and familiarity as the actual drug craving. The bathroom was the most common place for me to do a couple of bumps when I was out and about. It offered a quiet place away from the crowd where I could go into a stall, unfold my package, and take a snort undetected.

Being an experienced passer and user of cocaine in bathrooms, it's not hard to spot others with like intentions. One particular evening, shortly after I opened my third restaurant, NAWLINS, I went into the bathroom to relieve myself. Both urinals were occupied, so I waited politely until one gentleman was finished and went to the sink to wash his hands. I stepped up to the urinal to do my business. When I was finished, I noticed the other guy had not moved from the urinal and the first guy was still washing his hands. Strange, I thought, but gave it no more mind. As I walked around the guy to the sink, the first guy finished washing his hands and went back to the guy at the urinal and grabbed his hand. Gotcha! I knew a pass when I saw one.

Just as I was about to lay into these guys for doing drugs in my restaurant, the guy who just finished peeing reached out toward the wall behind the urinal and grabbed a white cane with a red tip. I slunk out of the bathroom just ahead of them. A minute later they walked out together. I watched the gentleman escort the blind man through the restaurant to the outside deck and to his seat at the keyboard with the band. I introduced myself during a break in between sets and we had a few laughs over the story. Danny Keen has been a steady musician at NAWLINS for three years now.

My continuing to drink alcohol while in an outpatient program breaks every definition of sobriety and every rule of every program. Total sobriety is what they preach. That's the only thing that works…alcohol is a gateway drug to much harder substances…blah blah blah. This is the tried and true method, for sure, but it was not to be my path. I enjoy a drink for the same reasons everyone else does. It makes me wittier and a much better dancer. But really, there is nothing like sipping a nice, thick, full-fruit Cab or Meritage, accompanied by a fatty piece of rib eye, seared on the outside and perfect blood-red and juicy on the inside. It's like heaven for me. My brain probably releases more serotonin and dopamine with a bite and a sip than if I smoked crack for 24 hours while eating dark chocolate.

I started drinking when I was growing up in and around the bars of southern Nassau County, Long Island, in the heydays of the Good Rats, Stray Cats and Twisted Sister, way before WLIR changed its format. Yes, if you do the math, you'll find I was around 16 when those bands were still playing in local bars like two of my favorites, Heckle and Jeckle's of Massapequa and Arrows in Bellmore.

I had my first drink in a bar called the Blind Pig on Merrick Road, somewhere between Wantagh and Massapequa. I ordered an apricot sour. I don't know if I was more shocked to be served or the bartender was more shocked that I actually ordered one of those, but he served it and I drank it. I don't even remember who I was with. Shortly thereafter, sniffing coke in the bar and ordering a drink became as commonplace as putting ketchup on a hamburger. It got to the point where I wouldn't go out without a package in my pocket. From the time I was 18 to well into my 40s, there wasn't a bar or restaurant I patronized without visiting the commode to bump up.

OVERCOOKED

To make it easier to do drugs in front of people without their knowledge, I got myself a bullet, a handy little gadget I purchased at the local head shop in The Sunrise Mall called Spencer Gifts. Not to embarrass them or be subject to a lawsuit from a nationwide corporation that makes its living selling novelties but NOT drug paraphernalia, Spencer Gifts did sell bongs and other items of interest to the casual drug user in the '80s

Shaped like a bullet, it was a plastic apparatus that screwed onto the top of a one-gram vial. It was translucent glass mini bottle, I assume, so users could see how big the hit packed into it was, something I never needed to view, as I always packed it to the max. With it hidden in my front pocket, I would hold it upside down to load the contraption by flicking my finger against the glass vial, shaking the powder down into the chamber, thus chambering a round.

As I pulled my hand from my pocket, I would twist the little lever on top, rotating the hit from on top of the vial around to the front of the bullet. Then with a smooth motion of my hand, I'd raise it to my nose and insert the end into a nostril, give a little sniff and whoosh, up shot the cocaine.

To the casual onlooker, it would appear as though I had merely rubbed my nose with my thumb and index finger. The bullet had a tiny—and I do mean tiny, lest some cocaine powder could fall out—weep hole or carb, as they say in the business, to allow air to enter the chamber as you sniff the coke out. This helped shoot the powder straight into my nasal cavity where my capillaries eagerly awaited to absorb the drug and rush it to my brain. Someone once described cocaine as having the ability to intensify everything about you. Which sounds about right, but what if you're an asshole?

After I perfected this move, I no longer needed to scurry into the bathroom to satisfy my addiction, unless I wanted to do a social bump with a friend or was trying to get my dick sucked by a female. Just thought I'd clarify that it was always a female, as you never know these days, not that there's anything wrong with that.

Somewhere along the line, I traded my bullet for a crack pipe and I no longer frequented bars. I graduated to the crack houses.

One of my biggest fears about falling off the wagon and using again has been the possibility of running into someone from my drug days in a bar or restaurant when my guard is down, weakened by alcohol, then ending up in the bathroom at the same time. But this fear has ended up being my greatest strength thus far. Being afraid has kept me clean.

OVERCOOKED

Ivan Sayles

Chapter Eleven

Lock and Load

My adopted mother, Ruby, had a sister named Cecile. Aunt Cecile lived with her parents in a two-story house, in a row of identical-looking attached homes in Brooklyn. She never married and continued living with Grandpa Joe after his wife, my grandmother Evelyn, died in 1968. We used to visit the house once a year or so, but after Grandpa Joe died in 1984, we never went back.

As I was starting 5th grade in September of 1972, my mom, Ruby, died of ovarian cancer. Shortly thereafter, Aunt Cecile came to Long Island to live with us and help my dad take care of my younger sister Eve and myself. She lived with us for a time but eventually moved back to Brooklyn when my father hired a live-in housekeeper. She was an African-American woman in her mid-40s, who I lost my virginity to at age 13. That's really all I want to say about that, so let's fast-forward 22 years.

On a hot July day in 1994, I got a call from the New York City Police Department, telling me there had been an accident at my aunt's and I needed to go to the house in Bay Ridge. I asked some questions, got some vague answers and was pretty much told to get my ass over there. I hadn't been to her house since the passing of Grandpa Joe 10 years earlier, and I had to buy a map —yes, a paper map from a gas station—so I could find the place.

When I arrived and met the police officers out front, I noticed from the sidewalk that the front door had been broken. I immediately put two and two together and got 10. Freaking out, thinking Aunt Cecile had been murdered, I leapt toward the front door and needed to be physically restrained from running inside. As it turned out, the next door neighbors had called the police because they hadn't seen my aunt in several days and there was a bad smell coming from the house. Cecile had passed away in her bed of a heart attack, and by the time I got there the police had broken in the front door and had already done their preliminary investigation, ruling out foul play.

As a young man, I saw the house differently than when I was a child, and once inside I was taken aback. Everything was as I remembered: the rugs, the furniture and the trinkets. But it was as if no one had touched anything since I was last there in my teens. I saw a neglected home typical of those of many seniors today who are separated from loved ones for whatever reason. It was a home once meticulously cared for, yet frozen in time from a date some 40-odd years ago when it and its owners' were in their prime. The home had aged in tandem with its inhabitant.

Maintenance on the house had stopped years ago, due to Cecile's physical or financial inability. The love for the home was still apparent: furniture was covered with blankets to hide the faded, worn upholstery, and perfectly placed doilies sat under trinkets on dusted tables. There was a white lace tablecloth on a dining room table set for no one, yellowed with time. It was dark and musty with many original fixtures and furniture dating back to the 1940s. I could literally feel the loneliness of the home.

As children, we were never allowed upstairs and it was always a great curiosity to Eve and myself to know what was up there. This made it a particularly surreal experience, walking up the creaking staircase behind a police officer to see my aunt's bedroom for the first time ever, to identify her body.

I had never seen a dead body before, with the exception of the few times I attended wakes and the bodies were prepared by trained experts. Veins are filled with embalming fluid to halt the body's decay and horrific smell that goes along with it. The body is laid out perfectly for viewing, head propped up on a pillow with plush fabrics lining the casket. The deceased is dressed in their Sunday best, face painted with peach-colored blush over thick makeup, transforming the pale grey skin into something we trick our minds into believing resembles that person when they were alive. Out of respect for my beloved Aunt Cecile, I will not describe the state I found her in. Suffice it to say she had been there for several days in an un-air-conditioned home in July.

It was then that I realized there is no dignity in death, there is only death. All that there ever was of our being, everything that makes us human—the soul, if you will—leaves our bodies with our last breath and what remains is just that, the remnant of a once-thriving human. There, in front of me in her bed, lay my aunt's remains. Her soul had left her body days ago. My aunt who had been capable of so much love, compassion and selflessness, was no more.

She loved my sister and me as if we were her own offspring. She spent a life of love and sacrifice for others, never marrying, taking care of her father, me and my sister. I feel regret in my heart for her, as I'm sure she never expected her beloved nephew to become a crackhead. So, it's in the second half of my life that I atone for my sins and try to live up to the standard that has been set before me by my wonderful family, a standard of honesty and integrity, so simple for the common person, but so far beyond my reach as an addict.

What does all this have to do with a gun? you might ask. After the commotion of the funeral and sitting Shiva for a week, it was time to clean up the house. I rented a dumpster and spent my days with my sister Eve and brother Adam, rummaging through two generations of personal effects. Oh yes, Adam and Eve. When my father got remarried, Myrna became my mom number three, and Eve and I got our new brothers Russ and Adam, and our sister Gayle.

One afternoon when Adam and I went to Cecile's, we found a broken window in the dining room and some things looked out of sorts, as if they'd been rummaged through. We boarded up the window and when we finished, I left an old bullet I had found in the house out on the table by the broken window as a warning. It was stupid, I guess, but when we returned in the morning, the board on the broken window was kicked in and the bullet was gone. Whoever it was had vandalized the dining room, breaking the glass in the china cabinet and damaging some furniture.

I had never felt so violated in my entire life. What I did next in reaction to the break-in ended up being one of the dumbest things I've ever done, but I was pissed and had no one to whisper logic into my ear. I drove to the only gun store I knew of, on Merrick Road in Seaford, Long Island, and bought a small-gauge pistol-grip shotgun—a Mossberg. No wait time. No background check. No 'Ivan calm the fuck down before you do something stupid' time. Nope, the only question I was asked was, "Will that be cash or credit?"

I called Adam and told him to bring the night-vision goggles. We'd be staying in Brooklyn that night and staking out the house. By the grace of God, no one showed up that night or the next or ever again. I don't know what twist of fate stopped whoever it was from coming back. Perhaps Aunt Cecile intervened? Who knows? What I do know is if they had come back I would have taken a life, and probably spent the rest of mine in jail.

Fast-forward several years and I was alone in my house, the very same one I had grown up in and purchased from my parents when I was 28. There I was, lying in their master bedroom, smoking crack. I had gotten into the habit of lying in bed, getting high, and loading and unloading the shotgun. I'd load it with three or four bullets, pump the slide and eject the cartridges one by one.

I had two kinds of shells: one was the traditional shotgun shell that most people envision, made up of tiny pellets called shot. As they leave the barrel of the gun, they spread out like a cone. If you're hit with one of these at very close range, it will make a fairly small entrance wound but cause some serious damage with all the pellets bouncing around your body. Depending on where you're hit, your prognosis may be quite grim. If you're a distance away and hit by this shot, your body will be bespeckled by anywhere from 100 to 300 tiny pellets, depending on the type of shell used. It's likely you'll survive, as these pellets lose their penetrating velocity quite rapidly.

The other type of shell is a slug. The 20-gauge shell my gun holds is equivalent to about a .45 caliber round. With much more velocity coming from the shotgun barrel than the shorter barrel of a handgun, you can imagine what would happen if hit by that at any range.

As time went by, I began playing more and more with the gun when I was high. One night I was lying in my bed, going through my traditional motions of loading and ejecting the shells. I would load three or four shells, rack the slide and a round would be ejected. When all the shells were ejected, I would point the gun somewhere on my body and pull the trigger, dry firing the gun: click! then reload and start again. I guess it was sort of a pussy's way of playing Russian roulette, knowing the gun wasn't loaded.

I'd start down at my toes, dry fire the gun, load and unload, fire, and work my way up my body. One night I took a break in my game, packed my stem with a nice rock and took a hit. As I slowly exhaled, I felt the euphoria of cocaine flowing through my veins. I realized the gun was lying across my lap and reached down to pick it up, left hand on the barrel, right hand on the pistol grip, with my thumb on the trigger. BAM! Holy shit! I jumped out of my skin, not yet realizing the gravity of what I had just done. The gun was across me, my lap acting like a tripod, keeping the barrel level, enabling a horizontal shot that sailed straight through two rooms, and cracking the front window of my house.

I had loaded the gun with shot, not a slug, so the hole in the wall from the bedroom to the bathroom was small. Across the bathroom, there was a much larger spray pattern; I could see where the individual pellets of shot went through the drywall. A few went clear through both walls of the bathroom and penetrated the bedroom wall. They sailed across the second bedroom, cracking, but not penetrating, the front window.

In another remarkable case of my really good-bad luck, I realized that had I loaded the gun with a slug instead of with shot, the slug would have easily penetrated both sheetrock walls and sailed through my front window right into the window of the house across the street.

How many times have you seen these words in the newspaper? "I didn't know the gun was loaded." The article usually ends in the maiming or death of someone innocent. Had that gun been pointed at my gut, they would have found me, just as they found my aunt, lying in bed all alone, having died a lonely death.

The threat of the gun taking my life or injuring me was more real to me than the threat of any harm I could possibly do to myself taking drugs. My solution after this terrifying incident was to stop playing with the gun while getting high. Because, why stop getting high? Genius.

Chapter Twelve

Arrest Number Two

A couple of months after my first arrest, I was in Queens to buy some crack with a girl whose name has long since faded from memory. None of my regular guys were around, so I drove to Queens with her to meet one of her dealers. I never liked buying drugs from people I didn't know, or getting them through a third party. Third party deals never work out, as someone is always trying to get the better of someone else, taking some out of the bag for themselves or worse, taking the money and never coming back.

We were parked outside a bar in Queens, waiting for her guy to come out. He was long overdue and I was cranky and hungry. I got out of the car to get some Chinese food and by the time I got back, the deal was done and we drove away. Once around the block, I pulled over to inspect the purchase, and wouldn't you know it, it was short. We got the dealer back on the phone and drove back around the block to the same spot. The dealer walked over to the car and we started arguing about the deal. Frustrated and seeing it was going nowhere, I decided just to get out of there and accept my losses before the scene escalated into something I could no longer control.

I pulled away from the curb, and as I approached the end of the block, from the corner of my eye I saw a white a van coming from a side street, bolting toward us. It made a U-turn, cut me off and slammed to a dead stop. I was so pissed at this asshole, I started yelling for him to get the fuck out of my way. Out of my periphery, I could see an excessive amount of movement but I didn't quite get what was going on yet. Then I hear the girl say, "Oh, shit!"

I turned my head to the left and looked out the driver's side window down the barrel of a gun. There were people screaming at me. The man holding the handgun had a goatee and was wearing a ski hat and black sweatshirt. It still hadn't sunk in that these were undercover cops who were staking out the bar that her dealer used as his office, which made us pawns in an undercover police sting. We managed to drive away the first time without getting stopped, but ironically we got pulled over when we went back to argue about the count, not when we actually bought the crack. But whatever, it really didn't matter: they found the drugs and we were arrested.

We were brought to the precinct, separated, searched and processed, then brought to Queens Central Booking. For me, the worst part of being arrested was not the treatment or the people I was locked up with, but the not knowing. They don't tell you anything, and if you ask questions you're told to shut up. I was disoriented, way out of my element. I knew I would be released eventually. I just didn't know when.

The sitting and waiting with no outside communication and no answers was miserable. Unlike Nassau County, Queens processes its criminals at night. What's-her-name and I got arraigned that evening by public defenders and were released on our own recognizance—or ROR'd, as they say. We took a cab back to the precinct where the police had parked my car, and we went home. We both had the same court date and made arrangements to go to court together, but it didn't work out. She didn't show for court and I don't know what happened to her. I never saw her again.

I hired a lawyer to the tune of $5,000 and was told I was lucky my crime was in New York City, because Nassau County was much harder on drug offenders, a fact I was soon to find out on my own despite the advice of counsel. After a few court appearances, I was sentenced to four days of community service, which consisted of wearing a bright orange vest and picking up garbage on the side of the roadways…and since it was winter, also shoveling snow off the sidewalks on the bridges over the Grand Central Parkway.

Getting off so easily gave me a rush of invincibility. I scheduled my days for community service, canceled and rescheduled my days, being too busy smoking crack to be bothered to do anything else. One day I even smoked crack during my community service while picking up garbage along the road. I was pretty fucked up at that point and on my second or third day of community service, I made it to Queens only to get high in the car and never get out.

About a month after that, I had the pleasure of meeting two New York City Police "Warrant Cops" when they came to my house to arrest me because I had failed to show up for community service. It took me six months to complete a four day sentence. I was in pretty bad shape.

OVERCOOKED

Ivan Sayles

Chapter Thirteen

Three Mistakes I Made When Buying My First Restaurant

While writing about my life, I've looked back and realized how much I love what I do. I was born to be in the restaurant business. It's in my blood, and it always has been. I see now what a perfect fit owning a restaurant is for me. I just didn't realize or appreciate it until I got clean.

In the spring of 1996, I was day trading and house flipping, which were the engines that created the cash to buy a restaurant. Before you go on a fact-finding mission, 1996 was before day trading. Looking back I can now call what I did day trading, but I had no idea that's what it was at the time. Every morning I got the Wall Street Journal, read it from cover to cover, then recorded stock prices in a composition notebook, looking for stocks with a large spread between the highs and lows in a single day. If I found one that tended to fluctuate significantly, I would buy it at the low end and hope to sell it at a higher price sooner than three days, which was when the money would be due for the purchase. It was time consuming and risky, to say the least, but I made money.

I had time for this, because my other main source of income was house flipping. After the housing market shot up in the '80s and then surprised everyone by crashing in the '90s, there were plenty of bank-owned properties on the market, so Vic and I did our best to capitalize on that. What's really shocking is that about 20 years later, the same thing happened again and people were surprised again, which lends truth to one of my Ivanisms A person is smart but people are dumb.

I was looking through a newspaper classified section and came across an ad for a waterfront restaurant. I was looking for residential real estate but I always scanned the business opportunity section, as well. I don't know what exactly caught my eye about the ad, but something did. I called the broker and went down to his office, got some more information, signed a confidentiality agreement and next thing I knew, I was on the Nautical Mile touring the Texas Ranger.

The Nautical Mile is a working waterfront community on the south shore of Long Island. It comprises about 20 restaurants and bars, two family owned fish markets (three before superstorm Sandy), bait and tackle stores, souvenir shops, commercial, charter and day-fishing boats, party boats, a marine gas station, public docking, mini golf, and depending on what year you visit, it may or may not have a gambling boat.

The area has been a working seaport and tourist destination for a good hundred years and has stood the test of time, going through its share of peaks and valleys, surviving numerous hurricanes and recessions, but always rebuilding itself and becoming better. I grew up just two towns away in Bellmore and worked 20 minutes away at Jones Beach but it was remarkable how little I knew little about the Mile.

I had been to its famous Freeport Festival a few times and gone flounder fishing on the original Captain Lou, a day-fishing boat and nighttime party boat. The only restaurant I had ever eaten in was the family-owned Crab Shack, which opened in 1978 and is still there today. Not too many restaurants are able to boast of being in the same location under the same family ownership for 40 years.

In 1996, age and years of neglect were showing their toll on the Mile. Crumbling sidewalks and potholed streets were not welcoming to tourists; deteriorating storm drains and collapsing bulkheads were causing frequent flooding; and many of the businesses were in desperate need of a facelift. The Texas Ranger was a long, narrow building covered in pale blue vinyl siding, looking more like a double-wide trailer than a restaurant. One great thing, among the many negative things I was unaware of during my negotiations to buy the Texas Ranger, was the plan by the Village of Freeport to revitalize the Mile.

In 1998 the Village did a massive improvement on the Nautical Mile, raising the streets and fixing the storm drains. They buried all of the power lines, installed 10-foot-wide brick sidewalks, and new lighting and benches along the whole block. Unbeknownst to me, I ended up purchasing a business in a beat-up area poised for renovation and expansion. All I had to do was survive my first two years.

As I get older I realize, the younger I was, the closer I was to knowing it all, and being a 29 year old graduate of the Culinary Institute of America, I figured I had the world by the balls, and no one could put one over on me...but they did.

When the timing was right between a full moon and high tide, the streets of the Nautical Mile would flood. Perhaps that's why they nicknamed it The Nautical Mile in the first place? If the streets happened to flood during business hours, well, that was the end of business hours. The cause of the high water is a very high "moon tide." The scientifics of it are complex, but suffice it to say, it's a three-day-long process occurring over a 2- to 3-hour period twice a day.

To add insult to injury, local television news had stock film footage of a guy driving a boat right down the middle of the street during high tide. If the high tide came in at 3 p.m., the streets would have flooded and then the water receded by 5 p.m. One might think, that's ok; at least we'll get the dinner crowd. Nope, because sure as shit, the 6 o'clock news on Channel 12 and WABC would broadcast the video of this guy in his dinghy powering up Woodcleft Avenue, as if it were live coverage. Bye bye dinner

Or they would show their reporter standing in the flooded street that was shot sometime in the morning. Not very responsible news coverage, in my opinion. I even wrote a letter to ABC, complaining about their van racing down the Mile, throwing such a wake it was causing damage to the shops along the street. Unfortunately, my research team, while doing their due diligence somehow missed this minor event, which only occurred about eight times a year. Definitely mistake number one. I'd met with the owners of the Texas Ranger, a son a daughter, we'll call them Peter and Patty, three or four times before I bought the restaurant...my appointments conveniently scheduled around the flooding.

On December 9, 1996, I bought the Texas Ranger, The Ranger's claim to fame, was the "Special Burger" or "Ranger Burger" as locals called it, a two ounce beef patty with a slice of tomato, cabbage, and "special sauce" which sold for 99 cents and quite famous in the local area, and of course, something I had never heard of.

Negotiating the deal took about six months. Not wanting to boast about buying a restaurant before I actually had a written contract, I kept my mouth shut and didn't discuss it with many people. Had I discussed it with a few friends familiar with Freeport and the Nautical Mile, I might have learned a few things about the flooding and the Special Burger, but I knew what I was doing, so why consult anyone?

During our six-month-long negotiations, I did make it a point to eat at the Texas Ranger a total of three times...and as my luck would have it, always at low tide. This was the extent of my business plan, due diligence, demographic and market research. Shrewd! In my three visits, I had sampled a steak sandwich, a seafood platter and fried clams. I was now confident and ready to negotiate the biggest deal of my life.

Ivan Sayles

Once the contract was signed and we were approaching the closing date, I began telling friends and family that I would soon be purchasing a waterfront restaurant on the Nautical Mile. They wished me good luck and couldn't wait for me to open. My brother Adam, on the other hand, had his own ideas and exclaimed, "That's great! Now, we can eat for free!" To my surprise, many of my friends had heard of the Texas Ranger and its "Special Burger." I didn't pay it much mind; anyone can sling burgers, right? Wrong again. Mistake number two.

At the closing, I asked Peter and Patty if I could retain one of them for a week or two to help ease the transition of ownership and introduce me to customers. No problem, they said, Patty agreed to stay on and help. Mistake number three.

One of the terms of the sale was that I could not purchase the property for two years. I didn't think much of it at the time, but I now realize what a smart move that was for the sellers. In an industry where seven out of ten restaurants fail in the first five years, the odds totally worked in their favor. Had I bought the business outright and failed in the first year, the bank would get the business. However, if I was renting the restaurant from them and I failed, they would get it back and could reopen it or sell it again, keeping every penny I had given them.

One of my plans was to modernize the look of the restaurant, particularly the hideous vinyl siding. I was not allowed to apply for a building permit until I had possession of the property. We had also agreed that I could use the Ranger name, logo and menu for the first few months, until I completed my renovations and changed the name to Rachel's Waterside Grill.

At the closing, I asked Peter about his menu mix. The menu mix is an important tool for any restaurateur it represents the amount of sales per menu item. For example, if you have 10 items on the menu and you do 100 covers, it's highly unlikely you'll sell ten of each item, as some items are obviously more popular than others. Your menu mix is the ratio of sales per item vs. items on a menu. This information was important in to order supplies and prepare the kitchen for opening day.

Peter told me that all items on their menu sold equally. I questioned his statement; it seemed highly unlikely, as some things are just more popular than others. But he assured me that indeed his menu had an even menu mix and I took him at his word.

I also inquired about the Special Burger, aka Ranger Burger and its special sauce. Peter told me the recipe for the sauce was a family secret and since they planned on starting a franchise with the "Special Burger," I couldn't have it. Oops! Another thing my research team missed. They were kind enough to give me the general idea of how it was made and of course, being a CIA graduate, I felt I would have no problem duplicating it...NOT.

This would prove to be a major blunder. I was just so trusting and naïve back then. It sucks to think that life's experiences have turned me bitter. I do believe that generally, people are good. But these two, as I figured out later, saw me coming a mile away and were salivating at the thought of making a meal out of me, keeping the $150,000 I had given them and taking the restaurant back. Another Ivanism I share with my partner Rich at key moments is, "We just got fucked. We've been fucked before. We'll get fucked again. We better fucking get used to it." Well, I had just gotten fucked.

The rest of the closing went ok. There were some last-minute arguments over small details, as there always are at closings, but in the end we reached a compromise: the sellers got what they wanted and it cost me more money. Perfect!

So, on a Monday morning, I signed the papers and bought myself The Texas Ranger. I immediately drove into New York City to pick up my liquor license, a wonderful way for the State of New York to welcome you into business and extract $2,500 from every restaurant, bar, catering hall, liquor store, 7/11, supermarket deli, etc. that sells alcohol. That's on top of collecting 4 percent of every dollar spent in the State and the cacophony of other taxes levied upon its lowly citizens. One day, maybe, someone can explain to me why we have trouble balancing the budget? Anyway, I picked up my license and headed back to Freeport to get ready for opening day: Tuesday, December 10, 1996, my 30th birthday.

Monday evening, I walked over to the restaurant next door, Otto's Sea Grill, to introduce myself to my new neighbors. I met Barbra, Arnhem and their daughter Ilona, whose family has owned Otto's since the turn of the century (the 20th century, that is.) They have their original liquor license from 1933, when prohibition ended, hanging on the wall to this day. They are wonderful, hardworking people who, for the past 23 years, I'm proud to call my friends and neighbors.

I introduced myself to Arnhem, who must have been around 70 at the time. He was a tall, charismatic man with white hair, piercing blue eyes and a befitting smile. I told him I had just bought the Texas Ranger next door. As Arnhem reached out and shook my hand to wish me luck, he began chuckling. I gazed at the smiling faces of his wife and daughter. Now I was really starting to get nervous. What had I done? Had I been duped? Had I bought the great albatross of Woodcleft Avenue?

As he chuckled, he began telling his story. He spoke with a faded but undeniable German accent and told me that years earlier, he had done a similar thing. He had gone next door to introduce himself to the new owners of the Texas Ranger, welcome them to the block and wish them good luck. Peter told him to fuck off and get off their property and that the Texas Ranger was going to put him out of business. That was the beginning of a feud between the two restaurants, that didn't end until I moved in next door. I soon realized their smiles and laughter was not at me, but because they were happy to get a new neighbor. I had just made my first of many friends on the Nautical Mile.

Needless to say, my first day as a restaurateur was a disaster. My theory of having Patty work with me to help with the transition was a huge misjudgment, as was listening to any of her ad-

OVERCOOKED

vice. I still have nightmares about opening day. Menu mix, my ass! My 1st day as a restaurateur was a beautiful sunny December day, we did 50 lunches. We sold 49 Special Burgers and got 40 complaints. I don't know if the other nine customers liked their burger or just were too polite to say anything. My bet is that they were polite.

We also sold one steak sandwich to my friend Vic, who sat at the bar, enjoyed his lunch and wished me luck. This torture went on for four days, while I listened to Patty's advice on how to make the customers happy and dealt with the myriad problems that go along with the opening of a restaurant.

Fortunately, the Texas Ranger had a loyal following and the customers kept coming in. By Friday, I was ready to pull my hair out. No one seemed happy with the food and I kept turning to Patty for advice, who happily dealt it out to me with false compassion and a smile like a professional hustler dealing cards from the bottom of the deck, assuring you your luck is bound to change. On the fourth day, one of my servers didn't show up, so now on top of all this I had to wait tables. They taught me how to wait tables in college but there's a very thick line between knowing how to do something and being good at it, and being a good waiter is something I'm not.

It was a disaster of a day. Customers were complaining about the food; no surprise there. I was trying desperately to keep everyone happy. Then there was Patty, up at the hostess stand, manning the helm of the sinking ship, smirking and basking in my frustration. One of the topping options for the Ranger Burger was chili. This involved ladling four ounces of chili right on top of the burger—bun and all. Patty had previously told me they didn't put meat in their chili. OK, I thought, the menu didn't say vegan chili but if that's the way they do it, fine. Who was I to argue? Vegan chili is commonplace on today's menus but not so much in 1996, In fact, Rachel's serves a vegan pasta Bolognese and we do quite well with it. She and Peter must have had a good laugh over that one.

Ivan Sayles

The dining room was full and I was failing miserably or in the weeds as they say. A customer had called me over to his table to scream at me—yes, scream—because there was no meat in his chili. As soon as I was able to retreat from the shit-storm he was raining down on me I back peddled over to a six-top I had been waiting on to see if they wanted coffee and dessert.

I don't know if you people realize how nasty some of you can be when it comes to your food. I know that's an unfair statement because 99 percent of you have the ability to communicate your issues in a civilized, polite manner, and in my experience most customer issues are legitimate and can be fixed very easily. To the other 1 percent, fuck you! And I mean that. Really? To scream at a server because they made a mistake and brought you the wrong salad dressing or something like that? As if it's ruined your life? Do you beat your children, too? What's wrong with you? Wait two minutes and we'll get you another one. Or holy shit, if it's going to be more than two minutes, we'll buy you a drink or a free dessert.

Anyway back to the six-top. "Dessert and coffee anyone?" I said with a smile. Uh oh, I could see it on the customers face here we go again. "DESSERT?" she yelled. "We've been waiting a half-hour and haven't even gotten our lunch yet!" She insisted on seeing a manager and as I was explaining that I was the manager, they'd had enough and walked out. My head was pounding. I felt like such an idiot. I was a mess. I couldn't focus on anything. For four days, all I was hearing was, "It's not the same," "It looks different," "It tastes different." I was having so many problems at this point, my problems were begining to develop problems.

When you buy a business, there's no test drive, no guarantee, and no "we're sorry you didn't like it, here's your money back" clause in the contract. It became apparent to me that Patty wasn't helping me at all. No, she was sabotaging me. I was waiting for permits to renovate the façade and they had agreed to let me use the Texas Ranger's name, but not its recipes.

OVERCOOKED

If I failed in that time or anytime in the first two years of our lease, they would repossess a newly renovated building and keep all the money I'd spent to purchase and renovate the place. The thought of them chomping at the bit, hoping for my demise, did nothing but strengthen my resolve for success.

As lunch that afternoon was coming to a close, one of the servers needed two cups of coffee. Unfortunately, there was only one left in the pot, Patty decided to show us a little trick and added hot water from the hot water spout on the coffee machine to the coffee pot to turn one cup into two. That was all I could take. I thanked her for all her help and told her I would no longer need her. Meanwhile I teach my staff to discard coffee that's been sitting too long and to always tell a customer when they're making a fresh pot, for two reasons, one, too buy a few extra minutes and two, who wouldn't be happy to wait an extra couple of minutes for a fresh cup?

Patty's consulting time was up, and so coincidentally, was the tide. I locked up after my fourth exhausting day, waded through knee-deep water into the parking lot across the street and got in my car. I debated on waiting until the tide went down, but I had a Chevy Blazer and what the fuck did I buy a 4x4 for, if not for moments like this?

I had no experience driving through floods and as I drove deeper into the water I gave the Blazer more gas figuring the faster I drove, the faster I would get out of the water. Wrong again, Ivan! Water started spraying outward from the car as I accelerated, then onto the front windshield, obstructing my view. A little more gas, a little more speed, and I'd be out of this in a second.

The tow truck driver was kind enough to let me sit in front with him for the ride to the service station and even dropped me at home. Within the hour the water had receded my car was at the station and I was in the tow truck on my way home. Patience has never really been my thing.

At this point, I was ready to stick a needle in my eye. But being an optimist, by the time I got home, I had convinced myself that getting water in my engine the same week I bought a restaurant was akin to being shit on by a really big bird: it had to be a sign of good luck. I decided my situation really couldn't get much worse than it was, so I felt pretty confident in my good luck theory.

I didn't sleep that night; my mind was on fire. I started thinking about Coke. Not the kind you put up your nose, believe it or not, but the soda. In 1985 with a major advertising campaign, The Coca-Cola Company decided to switch its nearly 100-year-old tried-and-true product, Coca-Cola to New Coke.

To say this move was a disaster is an understatement. Seventy-seven days after its introduction, due to public outcry, they pulled it from the shelves and reintroduced Coke Classic. But what did this mean to me? It meant, don't fuck with what people were used to. I couldn't give my customers the Ranger Burger. It just wasn't going to happen and there was the solution to my problem: I would stop selling it.

I called my kitchen crew and told them to come in at 8 a.m. I stayed up all night rewriting a new menu. Since there is no point in fighting a battle that can't be won, I was no longer going to try. When I was satisfied with the menu, I took a shower, drove to Restaurant Depot and waited out front until 7 a.m. when they opened. I got what I needed for my new menu, drove straight to the restaurant and started prepping with the guys in the kitchen.

That afternoon, we opened as Rachel's Waterside Grill and we're still here 23 years later! The sign out front still said Texas Ranger but the menu said Rachel's. It was my menu, my restaurant and from then on we were doing it my way. It was the proudest day of my life until Amanda arrived.

OVERCOOKED

Ivan Sayles

Chapter Fourteen

March 13, 2004 – Amanda

Everyone on the planet knows that parents love their children, but until you have a child of your own, you have no freakin' idea what that means. I cannot even begin to describe the emotions I had the moment she was born....

Although Amanda's birth was no surprise, her conception certainly was. I dated her mother, Veronica, broke up with and dated her again several times. We even tested the waters of cohabitation for a short period. My sister-in-law, Jess, best describes our relationship as that of fire and gasoline: a tiny spark is all it takes to set us off.

On paper, we looked like a power couple on the rise. It was 1999, the dawn of a new millennium. I had just purchased my second restaurant, while Veronica had recently been promoted to Assistant Vice President at a multi-state bank, which is a fancy way of saying she was the assistant to the assistant branch manager. At the time, the banking industry handed out vice president titles like vendors hand out peanuts at a ball game.

I have to say, if you walked into a branch with a complaint, seeing 'Assistant Vice President' on a name tag made you feel like you were speaking to the right person. In hindsight, I see that our relationship was nowhere near that of an up-and-coming power couple, but more like a powerful locomotive headed for derailment.

OVERCOOKED

Like most of my relationships up to that point, if you didn't drink alcohol and sniff cocaine, I wasn't interested in hanging out with you. I was thriving as a functioning addict, and our relationship was based on hard work and harder play, usually followed by a good solid fight. After about six months of turmoil, we decided it would be a good idea for us to move in together. Veronica gave up her apartment, as well as most of her furnishings and household possessions. As you might have guessed, moving in together didn't help our relationship one bit and six months later Veronica moved into her father's house.

In one year, she had gone from having her own apartment with kitchen, living room and bedroom furniture, to having nothing but a bed to sleep on at her father's. Yet somehow, we were both still under the illusion that our relationship might work.

One Sunday afternoon, in an attempt to patch things up, we took my boat down to Paddy McGees in Island Park. Paddy's was a well-known waterfront joint particularly popular for its Sunday afternoon happy hour with $5.00 lobsters. We were out to try and make things work, foolishly thinking an afternoon of fun and sun would cure all that ailed us. It didn't. It did bond us together for the rest of our lives. On that sunny Sunday in August of 2003, our daughter Amanda was conceived in a boat slip at the docks behind Paddy McGees.

I don't know if Amanda's mom and I were ever in love, despite trying to be, and realistically, I don't think it matters. But together we created an angel. That beautiful little girl we made together is the most special and wonderful thing I've ever known.

For the rest of August and September, we continued our normal life of working hard and playing harder. Then Veronica realized she was pregnant, so she stopped drinking, smoking and partying. I wasn't one of those fathers who changed his lifestyle along with the woman bearing his child: I was a dick.

I continued to go out drinking and partying every evening while she went to work in the morning and stayed home at night.

During routine checkups, we found out that her uterus wall was thin and she was told to take it easy. We were also told Amanda was a little small and the pregnancy needed to be closely monitored.

Pressure from her father, who at the time was not happy about his pregnant 34-year-old daughter living with him, pressure at work and pressure from dealing with me, coupled with some other complications, caused the doctor to tell her to stop working and spend the remainder of her pregnancy at home with plenty of bed rest, for fear of losing the baby. So, she moved back in with me. The rules had changed this time: we had separate bedrooms and we each came and went as we pleased. But since nothing with me is easy, I continued to pick fights with her, which added more unnecessary stress to the whole situation.

It was now December and Veronica really needed to get away from me to have some peace and quiet or she would lose the baby. Fortunately, my friend Vic and I owned a house in Southampton right across from the Shinnecock Hills Golf Course. Four bedrooms with a fireplace, pool and outdoor hot tub, nestled in a wooded area on a private road where we would often see deer and fox running across the front lawn was the perfect place for Veronica to convalesce.

I loved going out there, especially in the winter with snow on the ground. The best way I can describe a fresh snowfall in Southampton is: Mother Nature's way of temporarily soundproofing the world, allowing us to pause for a second and admire her beauty in picturesque silence.

Sitting outside in the hot tub, drinking a glass of wine during a snowfall is high on my list of perfect things to do, and the layout of the house just helped to enhance the experience. The hallway leading outside to the hot tub passed through the laundry room. We would take off our robes, put them in the dryer and then run barefoot on the snow-covered deck out to the hot tub, enjoy a relaxing half-hour or so sitting in the hot water, inhaling ice-cold air.

As we stood to go back inside, the cold air turned us into chimney stacks of steam from the water evaporating off our hot, half-naked bodies. OK, get that picture out of your mind; this is no "Penthouse Forum" sex story. I meant temperature hot, not hot sexy.

Visualize this: I was 5' 8" and 220 pounds of balding, pale white manflesh, so if you just threw up in your mouth, you might need to put the book down for a minute. We would walk into the house, grab a warm robe from the dryer and then sit by the fireplace. On a scale of 1-10, a night like this scores perfect!

The house was spacious, warm and secluded, and just what Veronica needed to relax for the remainder of her pregnancy, plus it got her away from me. She moved out to the Hamptons for peace and relaxation for the second and third trimester and I stayed in Bellmore and started fucking one of my waitresses.

It was March of 2004. Veronica was seven and a half months pregnant and she had been living in the Hamptons since December. She had stopped working, and she and her obstetrician were closely monitoring her pregnancy. It was now time for her baby shower, which, of course, would be at Rachel's. I closed the restaurant and set up for a nice Saturday afternoon brunch. Unfortunately, Veronica never made it.

As she was getting dressed for the shower, her water broke. Instead of brunch, Veronica went to the hospital to give birth to our daughter a month and a half earlier than expected.

I met her at the hospital soon after she got there. The room she was in was definitely not what I expected. I thought she would be in a standard single or double room, common at hospitals, and then wheeled into a delivery room when it was time to have the baby, but this was not the case. The birthing room, as I later learned it was called, was designed for the comfort of the mom. It was a spacious room for one person, with a bathroom, couch, several chairs and a TV. A sterile living room with a bed is how I saw it. I found out soon enough, it would also serve as the delivery room.

When I first walked in, it was organized chaos. Things were happening fast: pokes, prods, tests, nurses, nurses' assistants and doctors all fussing over Veronica. I had no idea what was going on, but everyone around us knew exactly what they were doing. The doctor was firing questions at Veronica: How often are the contractions? How painful are the contractions? Do you want an epidural? Oh, and by the way, we need to discuss the possibility of a C-section.

I loved it; Veronica not so much. In the middle of that mayhem, and much to my surprise, one of my all-time favorite movies, Willy Wonka and the Chocolate Factory, was on TV in the room. (It was the original, mind you, with Gene Wilder, not that counterfeit they tried to pass off with Johnny Depp.) I was in my glory!

I could have a baby and watch one of my favorite movies all at the same time. This was turning out to be a most excellent day! While Veronica was screaming out in pain from her contractions, I was shushing her and trying to get her to sing the Oompa Loompa song. Grinding her teeth, she scowled at me, "I don't wanna sing the fucking Oompa Loompa song!" Sometimes I can be a bit overwhelming.

The moment of truth was fast approaching. Veronica had suddenly become concerned about how all the drinking and partying we had done together in the first month or so, before she knew she was pregnant, had affected the baby. Now that we were approaching the final moment, she was getting nervous.

The doctor told us the baby looked OK—just small—and that's all we knew. Every time Veronica had a contraction, it was causing strain on the baby's lungs and since the contractions were getting stronger, there was more talk of a possible C-section if the situation got worse before Veronica dilated enough to have a natural birth.

OVERCOOKED

They gave her an epidural and when she was ready, the nurses moved her to the birthing area on the other side of the room. One of the nurses then kindly pointed out that there would be a chair behind me, if I needed it. Needed a chair? "For what?" I asked. I was so amped up I was bouncing off the walls. No way was I was going to sit down for this.

She said, "You know, in case you need to sit." "Why would I need to sit?" I asked. This was the most exciting moment of my life! I would have pulled Amanda out myself, if they allowed it. She said, "Well, in case you feel, you know, queasy...in case you feel faint." Faint? You mean some fathers pass out during childbirth? Inconceivable!

Meanwhile, I had been secretly hoping for a C-section, imagining how cool it would have been to see that. Pass out, my ass. I came to the hospital fully prepared to cut the umbilical cord and had even brought a camera to document the whole thing. This was the most exciting day of my life. No freakin' way I was going to pass out and miss it.

I didn't faint but I did choke. I was so excited, I never got one picture and I missed the whole cord-cutting thing. The birth just went too quickly: first the head crowned, then two seconds later, vwhoosh! She slid right out. Umbilical cord cutting time came and went in an instant, and the camera never left my pocket. It was 6:15 in the evening on March 13, 2004, even though on her birth certificate it says 6:15 a.m. Just like that, we were parents.

From the time Veronica's water broke until the time she gave birth was all of seven hours. I think I was still looking around the floor, trying to pick my jaw up when they handed me this blueish-purple, tiny, smooshed-face, three-pound, three-ounce baby girl. This had now taken over as the proudest moment in my life.

As I was standing in awe in the brightly lit hospital room holding my less than one-minute-old daughter, Veronica asked me in a soft, quivering voice, "Is she OK?" I would imagine that even with a smooth pregnancy, there is a moment of anticipation, a moment of simultaneous joy and fear at that second of delivery, a moment of panic and prayer, hoping everything is all right. I couldn't fathom what was going on in Veronica's head right then.

I looked down at Amanda, now cleaned off and tightly wrapped in a little blanket. The nurse covered her head with a tiny cap. I always thought newborns were ugly and never understood how people could call them beautiful, and ooh and ahh over them. Not anymore. I had never in my life seen something so beautiful. Her eyes were closed and as I raised my hand over her face, it cast a shadow over her head. Amanda, now going on two minutes old, opened her eyes for the very first time. The pride of being the first human being she ever saw was all mine.

We were suddenly all alone in the room, just me and Amanda, the only two people on the entire planet. All alone in a crowded, brightly lit, noisy room. For an instant, time stood still, and everything else just faded away. As I moved my hand away from her face and the light glared into her eyes, she closed them. I kept hearing this faint voice in the background, "Is she OK? Is she OK?"

I moved my hand back over her face and cast a shadow over her eyes. That faint voice in the background was getting louder. "Is she ok?" Amanda opened her eyes again. At that moment I knew she was fine. It was a feeling that came from deep within my soul. When she looked up for the second time, I knew beyond the shadow of a doubt, I knew she was absolutely perfect. As the world around me started to reappear and come into focus, I realized Veronica was screaming at me. "IVAN! IS SHE OK?"

"She's perfect," I said in a whisper at first. "She's perfect," I replied again. Suddenly, I was back in the crowded brightly lit room.

"How do you know?" Veronica asked.

"Because, I do," I said. God blessed us with a perfect three-pound, three-ounce little girl. I couldn't explain it to Veronica in any other way except, "I just know."

My sister Gayle had given birth to my niece Dalya eight days before Amanda was born. When I went to the hospital to visit her and held Dalya in my arms, she was less than a day old. She was the tiniest baby I had ever held, until Amanda. Dalya weighed seven pounds, twice Amanda's size. The entire length of Amanda's arm from shoulder to fingertip was the length of my pinkie.

She would spend a month and a half in the Neonatal Intensive Care Unit, until she was big enough and strong enough to leave the hospital. Veronica and I made sure one of us was there every two hours to feed her for the entire time she was in the NICU. She was so small that when I walked by the nursery and saw all the newborn babies lined up, all I could think was, "Damn, those kids are huge!" That first night in the hospital, she was put in an incubator with all kinds of IVs and monitors hooked up to her. She needed oxygen tubes in her nose to help her breathe.

The next morning when I arrived, the oxygen tubes were gone. Somewhat freaking out, I questioned the nurse about why they were no longer in her nose when I'd been told she needed them. The nurse said that every time they put them in, Amanda would pull them out, so they stopped trying. She was definitely her father's daughter!

It took you just a short time to read this chapter, but it took me three days to get it on paper, followed by countless rewrites. As I reminisced about that spectacular afternoon I spent in the hospital with Veronica, welcoming our daughter into this world, writing about it has been a bittersweet experience that brought me to tears many times.

How could I let myself do it? God had given me the most wonderful gift in the world, my beautiful baby girl. I love her so much and yet within two and a half years, my need for smoking a glass pipe would become more powerful than the love I had for that precious new baby.

Veronica was now a full-time mother. Her days of drinking and partying were over and she got down to the business of raising a little girl. I, however, went in the opposite direction, continued with my drug use, progressively getting worse, and going from functioning drug addict to dysfunctional junkie. I would come within inches of losing everything—my family, my business, my home, my daughter, my life.

Amanda was the catalyst to the greatest gift of all, but it would be almost seven years before I could overcome my demons, come back from hell, and be given a second chance to experience her for the first time, all over again.

OVERCOOKED

Chapter Fifteen

Busboys

Being a male member of the human species myself, I can say with firsthand experience that there is nothing stupider on the planet than a young man between the ages of 16 and 20. It has to do with the dreadful combination of testosterone overload and knowing everything there is to know about everything and having absolutely no clue about anything all at the same time.

If there is a decision made by a young man, it's usually the wrong one. I don't know how any of us survived into adulthood. Unfortunately, this gender and age group is the primary workforce pool for busboys. One would think these young men would be hard working, full of energy and enthusiastic about earning cash, but for the most part, one would be wrong. About 20 percent of our busboys are sharp thinkers and hard workers, but they don't last long. They're destined for better things, be it moving up to a server position or moving onto something else entirely.

Most of my employees have been with me for years, yet we have a revolving door when it comes to busboys. I prefer to see busboys working a couple of shifts before I bother to ask their names, but sometimes their stupidity is revealed before I even get the chance to do that. For example, one evening I was standing at a table talking with some regular customers and I saw this half-wit walking toward me through the dining room, holding a saucer and cup of coffee. As he approached the table, he took a sip of his coffee, interrupted my conversation and asked, "Excuse me, but I couldn't help noticing you walking around the restaurant today and was wondering if I could get your name." Buh bye!

I'm thinking that by the time a child has reached puberty, their parents might have taken them out to eat once or twice and they might have picked up a few pointers from the experience… or not. Walking into the kitchen one afternoon, I saw another genius (who just recently stopped tying his shoes in double knots) walking toward me with something wrapped in foil that I assumed was the remains of a meal a customer didn't finish and wanted to take home. My instinct told me something didn't look right.

I asked him what he had in his hand. "A woman didn't finish her pasta and wanted to take the rest home." I reached out and grabbed the tin foil. This idiot took the china bowl we served the pasta in, put foil over it and was bringing it back to the table. I suggested to him that we give her some of our silverware, too, so she'd have something to eat with when she got hungry later.

Apparently he didn't get my sarcasm and thought that was a good idea. Had this kid's father been around to hear what came out of my mouth as he turned to get the silverware, he would have laid me out. Oh well, another one bites the dust.

Owning a restaurant on the water has its perks, including a free boat slip to keep one's boat in. In case you don't know, the word BOAT is really an acronym for "Bust out another thousand." Anything you need for a boat is way more expensive than it needs to be: nuts, bolts, hinges, screws, whatever, including gas that averages about a dollar a gallon more than for your car. They say the two happiest days of a boater's life are the day he buys a boat and the day he sells it.

The back deck of Rachel's overlooks my boat slip and serves as an overflow dining area/ employee dining room and smoking lounge. As I walked out onto the dock one Sunday afternoon to check the lines on my boat, I saw a cigarette butt on top of my brand new $2,500 canvas cover. As I got closer to examine the damage to the canvas, I saw that it was not a butt when it was tossed, but half a cigarette, as it had burned an inch-long canal in the canvas while it smoldered to extinction.

To say I was furious would be a gross understatement of my emotional state of mind. I immediately had my partner, Rich, and manager, Clare, launch a full investigation into the incident, checking everyone who was working, trying to match the butt to the smoker.

Smoking anywhere on Rachel's property was immediately forbidden and someone was paying for a brand new canvas and it wasn't going to be me. The word was out: I was on the warpath. After interrogating everyone working that shift, we narrowed it down to a prime suspect, a busboy. He wasn't scheduled for work for another two days, so I waited, seething. Tuesday afternoon, as his shift was approaching, my blood started to boil. I wanted to beat the crap out of this punk, but not wanting to go back to jail, I was prepared to settle on a verbal assault the likes of which he'd never experienced before.

The moment had arrived and he came walking toward me, head hanging low, not able to look me in the eye. He had clearly gotten wind of the situation and in a soft, nervous voice he said, "Ivan, I have something to tell you." Immediately, my heart started to soften. He told me he had tossed the cigarette onto the canvas by accident. He said he was sorry, offered to pay for canvas and said I could withhold the money from his salary until it was paid off. I was taken aback by this young man's honesty and integrity. Now what the fuck was I supposed to do?

The kid made $5.00 an hour plus tips. The next morning, he brought the canvas up the block to one of the boat canvas stores on the Nautical Mile and got a round patch to cover the hole for $35.00. I imagine if I had done the damage myself, that's probably what I would have done. My cheap ass wouldn't have bought a whole new canvas, that's for sure.

Now when I get on the boat and see the patch, I'll sometimes tell the unlucky soul who's with me the story of how it got there, even though I know they've heard it before. But telling it reminds me that no one is perfect and that there are good honest people out there. You just have to rummage around a bit to find them.

Chapter Sixteen

Arrest Number Three

The third time I was arrested was less than four months after my first arrest. One warm July night (or should I say early morning), Wayne, a fellow druggie, and I, had gone on a run. It was a warm, sticky morning around 3:30 a.m. We drove west along Jerusalem Ave. from the white, middle-class neighborhood of Bellmore, into the not-so-white, not-so-middle-class neighborhood of Hempstead, only to return along the same road in the opposite direction within minutes.

Now, I'm no detective, but it doesn't take much of a genius to figure out what two white guys are doing driving into the ghetto at 3:30 a.m. and returning 10 minutes later. As we were getting pulled over, I tucked the bag of crack under my foot in my sandals. Unbeknownst to me, Wayne had previously attempted to alter the registration sticker on his front window because it was expired. No sooner than the officer aimed his flashlight on it, we were sitting on the sidewalk in handcuffs watching the cops search the car.

I took that opportunity to break up the bag of crack and rub it into the ground with my sandal, which was working out fine until the cops found a jar of pills in my laptop bag in the back seat. I had Oxy, Xanax, Vicodin, you name it. I didn't use any of those pills myself and never thought of the consequences of being caught with narcotics that were not prescribed to me. I ended up getting locked up for drugs I didn't' even use. I had them with

OVERCOOKED

me in case some crack whore pill-head would get anxious in the middle of a drug and sex soiree. I would be the hero and have a pill handy.

I got away with the crack and got busted for the pills. The deeper I got into my addiction, the more risks I took to get my fix…and the more I got away with, the more invincible I thought I was. I was traveling down the road of the stereotypical drug addict. I had lost my license, gotten arrested and would soon lose my car, my friends, my family, and just about everything else. I had become the textbook addict

Ivan Sayles

Chapter Seventeen

I ♥ NY

There's nowhere else in the world I'd rather live than on Long Island. I make this statement without hesitation. I've visited many countries in four of the seven continents, the two other North American countries, a few in Central America, countless islands in the Caribbean, including Fidel Castro's, along with 18 states in the U.S. My roots are here; Long Island is my home, and I love it.

I love to travel. I want to experience other cultures and see life through the eyes of different people. I'll do the tourist thing for a while, but can't wait to get away from "the strip" and experience how the locals live. The last thing I'm going to do is visit a Planet Hollywood in every city in the world. If I wanted that, I have one right here in my beloved Manhattan.

I've seen my share of duty-free crap, t-shirt shops, snow globes, and key chains. However, I do make it a point to visit a McDonald's in every country I visit. After all, you can take the American out of America.... Anyway, I go for several reasons. McDonald's is my barometer for world currency standards; once I've compared what a Big Mac costs in pounds, euros, or pesos to U.S. dollars, it's much easier for me to convert local currency in my head. If a beer in a Mexican bar is 22,000 pesos and a Big Mac is 30,000, I know I'm in the ballpark of a fairly priced pint. Plus, I've eaten things in McDonald's that we don't have in the

U.S., like hot dogs, fried chicken, Tex-Mex burgers, pizza, lobster rolls and even The McArabia.

Guess what else foreign McDonald's have that we don't? Employees who actually take pride in their work. How refreshing is that? It's nice to be served with a genuine smile and asked how you enjoyed your meal as you leave, instead of being asked if you want to add an apple pie to that order. And guess what? That shit is contagious. It makes other people take pride in what they're doing and somehow through all that, politeness manages to weasel its way in.

Has a stranger ever given you a friendly look and said good morning to you as you got your coffee at 7-11, and have you returned it with an uncomfortable smile figuring they must have thought you were someone else? Well maybe, jackass, just maybe, they were being polite. Try it one morning. Greet a complete stranger with a smile and hello. You'll be surprised at how you'll feel better yourself for doing it. One thing I have to say about us New Yorkers is we are a rude bunch.

There was a school crossing guard who worked on the corner a few blocks from Rachel's, whom I drove by for years. I never stopped to say hello, and I'm certainly not anyone relevant in her life. She smiled and waved good morning to every car that drove past. But it's the way she did it that was special. As I drove to work, listening to only the thoughts in my head, oblivious to the world around me, the genuineness of that crossing guard's smile, her white-gloved hand waving at me and the goodness of her heart penetrated through the glass and steel surrounding me. No matter how foul my mood was before I passed her, I'd walk into work with a smile. What amazing power this woman had. What amazing power we all have.

I've only been to Jones Beach a handful of times since I worked at the Boardwalk Restaurant back in the '80s, yet it's sort of my security blanket, knowing it's only 10 minutes away and I can go there any time. Often when traveling east, I'll first drive south and take the 15-mile-long Ocean Parkway running parallel to the beach. It's a beautiful drive with the Atlantic Ocean on my right and the State Boat (Reynolds) Channel leading to the Great South Bay on my left, finally crossing the northern span of the majestic twin bridges of the Robert Moses State Parkway leading back to the mainland. It takes me a few extra minutes, but boy, is it worth it.

I can't imagine myself ever not living near the ocean. I wake to beautiful sunrises across the canal and seagulls squealing their morning protests. My feelings for Manhattan are the same. I am grateful to have been able to experience both the underground mall and top of the Twin Towers before 9/11.

I visited the Statue of Liberty for the first time as a child on a school field trip; same with the Empire State Building. It's been way too long since I went to a museum or Central Park, but knowing they're close by is priceless and reassuring for me. When people from out of town ask how far away I live from New York City, I explain that it varies. I live anywhere from 30 minutes to three hours away, depending on traffic, and 53 minutes to two hours away via the Long Island Railroad, depending on power failure, track work, miscellaneous delays or suicide on the tracks.

Jen and I go into "The City" a few times a year for much-needed adult time to enjoy a concert or Broadway show, or sometimes we go with the kids for family fun. On one of those memorable adult weekends, we checked into our room and stopped at the champagne bar in the lobby of The Plaza for afternoon cocktails followed by dinner. It was just what the doctor ordered. We had a great afternoon.

We didn't stay at the Plaza, mind you, we stayed at the Holiday Inn around the corner, but we certainly lived the life that day. After we ate, we went for a stroll along "The Park," or Central Park, if you're not familiar with the landscape. Jen suggested we go for an after-dinner drink and maybe some role-play fun. Role play? Fuck yeah! You don't have to ask me twice.

OVERCOOKED

We decided that Jen would go into a bar first and sit alone; I'd get in a fight with my "girlfriend," (a stranger I picked out of the crowd) and then go over to Jen and try picking her up. Cool, right? Jen walked into a restaurant that just so happened to be perfect for our scenario. It had a rectangular bar and as I walked in I saw her and positioned myself next to a couple sitting on the other side of the bar from her. I bought them a drink and explained that my wife and I were out having fun and asked if they could help me out. "Sure, no problem," they said. I bought two shots and then, being a gentleman, the boyfriend stepped back to enjoy the show.

His girlfriend and I knocked back the shots and she said very loudly to me, "So you think you're all that?" I retorted with an even louder, "Fuck you!" I turned and walked away. She shouted out after me with her very best New York City accent, "Why don't you go fuck yourself!"

Not bothering to look back, I gave her a NY City salute with my middle finger and continued on to the second act of my Broadway debut and walked around the bar to Jen. Just as I was starting to say hello, two bouncers grabbed me by the arms and escorted me out the front door. I watched Jen as she sat at the bar and literally spit her drink out, shaking violently up and down with laughter as I was dragged out.

Chapter Eighteen

My First Christmas

Being raised Jewish, I had no firsthand experience with Christmas trees, save seeing them for sale at Home Depot or on street corners. However the short time Veronica and I lived together before Amanda was born encompassed a Christmas, and she had insisted on having a tree.

I've always liked the way houses look decorated for Christmas, and was excited to do it myself for the first time. I have to say, I really enjoy the holiday season. Everyone is in a better mood because they're thinking about how they can make someone else happy, instead of thinking about themselves. Strangers smile and wish each other well. Why can't we do this the other 10 months out of the year? Maybe it has something to do with spending money you don't have on the people you care about the most, who knows? I'd love to shake the hand of the marketing genius who decided the best way to celebrate the birth of Christ and the Festival of Lights is to decorate our homes and give out presents. But if that's what it takes to make the world a happier place in November and December, I'll take it.

Every one of my siblings has married a Catholic, so we celebrate Christmas and Chanukah, and like most Americans, we refer to this time of year as "The Holidays," not so much to be politically correct, but because it's practical.

Veronica asked if I wanted to go fake or real. Suddenly, I was faced with my first Christmas decision: I was 39 years old and

I'd be damned if my first Christmas tree was going to be a fake. You couldn't get me to put a real tree in my house now on a bet, but the first one had to be the real McCoy.

We went to the local nursery; I wasn't buying my first Christmas tree from a truck on the side of the road. They had some display trees and the rest were wrapped up in netting, ready to go on top of a car. We were assured the ones wrapped up were the same shape and size as the ones on display. Veronica took the lead and looked around the lot for the perfect tree. When she finally found one, I thought it was a little large and voiced a quiet protest, stating that since this was my first, maybe we should start small and work our way up. That was immediately shot down. This was the right tree for us, and on top of the car it went. What I didn't know at that moment as we were driving away with the tree on the roof, was that the best part of my first Christmas experience was already behind me.

A tape measure would have been a good thing to bring shopping with us, I remember thinking as we struggled with the tree, still in its mesh, forcing it through our home's front door. Pine needles were shooting in every direction as we scraped the tree through the door jamb and into the hallway. You would think we would have cleared a space for the tree beforehand, because that would have been the smart thing to do. I've always been a "ready, fire, aim" kind of guy and this situation was no different.

After I cleaned up all the pine needles on the front stoop and in the hallway, we rearranged all the living room furniture to find the perfect place for the tree. I cut open the netting and this thing practically exploded. Pine needles were now everywhere again. There was this monstrosity of a tree lying on its side in the middle of the living room. I turned to Veronica and asked, "What do we do now?" She said, "You put it in the stand." "What stand?" I asked. Out the door and into the cold I went to buy a stand for the tree, seriously doubting if I had made the right decision to buy a live tree.

After a couple of bottles of red wine, some fruit and cheese and trimming off some branches and a couple of feet of trunk, we got the tree mounted and the pine needles vacuumed. It was now 1 a.m. and we were exhausted. We went to bed and just as I was drifting off to sleep, I was startled awake by a tremendous crash. The tree had fallen down on top of the coffee table. There were broken wine glasses, plates, cheese and grapes rolling around all over, not to mention plenty of pine needles everywhere.

As the Christmas season progressed, Veronica and I slipped back into our usual mode of bickering, disagreeing and generally not getting along. We never made any progress decorating the tree after reorienting it upright in the stand that first night. It just sat there dehydrating for three weeks, and fell down two more times. We spent that Christmas Eve at my sister Eve's house, celebrating with her, her husband, kids and the rest of the family. It was snowing pretty hard out and we had a bit of a drive, so we left early.

We were getting along for the moment; we had a nice night and were both in a good mood. Veronica suggested we get rid of the tree, clean up the house and maybe do some rearranging. We decided to get a jumpstart on the New Year, give the house a new look, and promised to try harder to make our relationship work. Great idea, but what would we do with the tree? Veronica wanted to put it out at the curb but I wanted no part of that. This was the house I grew up in. I'd known my neighbors all my life and there was no way I was tossing my first Christmas tree out on the curb on Christmas Eve.

I came up with the plan. Between the raging snowstorm and it being a holiday, no one was out driving around, so we threw the tree on top of the Pathfinder and slowly drove off. A few blocks away I found a nice spot by the woods near the parkway. I sped up, spun the wheel and slammed on the brakes. The truck responded precisely and whipped around, doing a 360 in the snow. The tree flew off the roof and rolled into the woods. It was a perfect landing and we drove home high five-ing each other and laughing.

When we got home, we started cleaning and rearranging. We called friends and family to wish them a Merry Christmas. I called my partner, Rich, and told him the story of our Christmas tree. We had a good laugh and since it was still early, he and his wife invited us over. We chose instead to stay home and clean up the mess. After a few hours and several furniture rearrangements, we decided to try to move the television from one side of the room to the other. This was a bit more of a project than I was looking for at the time, and it involved going outside to find out where the cable wire comes into the house.

I went upstairs and changed out of my comfortable flannel pajama pants and threw on jeans and a sweater. As I was pulling up my snow boots, Veronica opened the front door and started screaming bloody murder. "Oh my God! Ivan, oh my God!" I couldn't imagine what was going on.

I came stumbling down the stairs with one boot on to see Veronica standing in the doorway with her hand over her mouth, eyes wide open. There on my front stoop, jammed under the soffit was the fucking tree! Veronica was freaking out, "Oh my God, one of the neighbors must have seen us dump the tree!" But I knew better. Fucking Rich had gotten me again! I found out later that he and his wife, in the middle of the snowstorm, had gone out and stolen a Christmas tree off of a lot and put it on my front stoop.

Chapter Nineteen

Recovery

My second serious attempt at recovery started in November of 2008, with the help of my best friend, Eddie. I checked into an in-patient recovery center for the standard 28-day program. Great opening lines for the chapter in my book called "Recovery," right? Well, not so much. After three days, I walked out of the program and got on a bus to Manhattan.

As an employee of the federal government, my friend Eddie was able to arrange for me to get into a very prestigious and reputable rehab center in Pennsylvania called Monmouth. Eddie, by the way, should be writing his own anecdotal book about his years of flipping burgers and bartending in the restaurant and bar industry, and his dedicated service in federal law enforcement. But since you're reading my book, please allow me to recount one of my favorite Eddie stories.

Working for the FBI and stationed in Puerto Rico in the early '90s, Eddie and his partner were assigned to watch an individual who was a cab driver. Once the suspect was on the move, this presented quite a challenge, as taxis all look pretty much the same. Eddie's rookie partner suggested the very cliché move of knocking out a taillight to make the cab easier to spot in traffic. But Eddie had a better idea and told the greenhorn he'd be right back, and went across the street to Plaza de Las Americas.

Returning with a can of spray paint, he casually walked up to the taxi and spray-painted "Fuck You" in nice, big, fluorescent orange letters on the trunk. When he got back to his car, he said to his partner, "Now we'll have no problem following him in traffic!" I understand this did not go over well with his supervisors, but hey—Eddie always marched to the beat of his own drum.

Federal law enforcement agencies do not sanction rehab centers, kind of like police precincts do not sanction bars. But if you walk into a bar on Long Island where most of the guys have short hair and there are orange license plates with only three numbers hanging on the walls, you can bet the pints are ice cold and the cheeseburgers are juicy. So with that crooked logic, if this was the rehab federal law enforcement agents chose, I felt it was going to be a quality operation.

Looking back on my short time at Monmouth, I wouldn't say I'm bitter about the experience, even though I may sound critical of the place. One of the traits of addiction is that everything is everyone's fault but your own. When I left, I blamed Monmouth for my failure, when the truth of the matter was, I just wasn't ready for rehab yet. Sadly, I didn't see it that way at the time.

As good as the Monmouth program is, I consider these 28-day in-patient programs somewhat of a scam. Like Eddie says, "Nothing is legit." I don't mean the program is a scam in the sense that they don't provide a service and don't help people who want to recover. They do, but it's a scam in the sense of what they allow the public's perception to be.

Make no mistake, private rehab centers are businesses, particularly the ones you see advertised on television—the ones that look like resorts. They are businesses that exist for one purpose: to make money. Even not-for-profits need to make money. They have mortgages, electric bills, CEOs, directors, staff, doctors, accountants and lawyers that all need to be paid.

Business is business, addiction is addiction, and rehab centers are in the business of addiction. Advertising messages portray them as caring and dedicated to your recovery and how important your privacy is. That's a load of crap. There was plenty of name dropping, when they told us at Monmouth in group therapy sessions the names of celebrities who have been through their facility, as if to point out, "If so and so can do it, you can too," privacy and confidentiality laws notwithstanding.

The standard one-month in-patient rehab program is actually only 28 days. That's pretty close to a month. In fact February is 28 days 3 out of every 4 years. Why 28 days? It's an even four weeks. But when you do a little math and divide 365 by 28 you get 13. There are thirteen months in a rehab year...not 12 like the rest of us use. This ensures the rehab centers (that charge plenty for their services) get an extra month's payments every year. After all, this is America and in America you must always turn a profit, no matter how noble the cause. Addiction in the United States is thriving and the beauty of the addiction business is that it's not susceptible to recession, market fluctuation, unemployment or a falling housing market; the more depressed the economy, the more it thrives.

Many people abuse drugs and alcohol and when it finally comes to a head and starts affecting their jobs and spouses enough, they "go public." They confess to their drug or alcohol abuse, say they're sorry and agree to go to a one-month program. This is extremely common with blue-collar workers, and civil servants who have excellent health insurance coverage to pay for these programs. The programs are not as popular for the poor or uninsured that also desperately need them.

The insured middle-class addicts come out of rehab 28 days later, absolved of sins, and return to their families and jobs with a clean slate. For many of them, the only thing the program did was keep them clean and sober for 28 days. It did not cure their addiction. Again, I'm not saying that these programs don't work, as I wouldn't be writing this book had I not successfully completed one. But it's up to the individual to want it, not to be forced to go, in order to keep his job or marriage.

I've seen people who have been to six or eight in-patient facilities and still go back to using. One last thought on the business of rehab: you would think that the single best form of advertising for a drug or alcohol rehabilitation program would be its success rate, yet no one publishes it. Why not? Because it's astonishingly low. About 95 percent of crack addicts do NOT recover, but that fact doesn't fill beds.

I wish I could write more about my experience in this program, but truth be told, I don't remember much. What I do remember is being scheduled for pickup at my home at 8 a.m. and taking my last hit of crack at 7 a.m., hopping in the shower, packing my bag and getting into the car for the ride to Pennsylvania. I had been up for days and fell asleep as soon as we hit the parkway.

When I arrived, we did my admission paperwork. I got a physical and a pamphlet of schedules, rules, and regulations. It was a coed facility, but talking to the opposite sex was forbidden. The only time we saw the women was at meals and in group sessions that involved the entire facility. I went to my room and passed out.

When I was awakened, it was time for breakfast, followed by my first group session. I'll call it a small group, with about eight people. After that, it was time for a medium group meeting with about 20 people, then an individual meeting with my counselor, a short break, lunchtime, and then a large group meeting. I got some time to myself to contemplate the meaning of life, another individual session with a different counselor, dinner, more sessions and finally bedtime. It was like being at a 14-hour AA meeting. After three days, I walked out and took a bus back to New York. I came home confident I could do this on my own. The regimented atmosphere and discipline was just not for me. I was arrested again within three months.

Thinking we could control our addiction, some of my crack-smoking buddies and I came up with a few plans on how we could accomplish this. A particular favorite of mine is the one where we planned to work three weeks in a row, and then take off one week a month to go on vacation somewhere, smoke crack all week and then go back to work. This was a viable plan in our minds because the money we would make and save by not smoking crack for three weeks would more than fund the expense of getting on a plane to fly to an island in the Caribbean to smoke crack for seven days.

We never really got to the logistics part of smuggling the drugs and paraphernalia in and out of the country, or made any other sort of progress on the plan except dreaming about it. Sounds pretty stupid, right? That's because it is pretty stupid. Plus, if I got caught smuggling, it would have raised my legal issues to a whole new federal level. In our drug-clouded minds, it seemed like a perfectly good plan to assimilate our drug use into everyday normal life.

This fooling myself into thinking I could manage the unmanageable went on until August of 2009 when I went to jail. I had gone to my share of AA and NA meetings and had periods of sobriety lasting from a couple of days up to three weeks, but I always found my way back to the pipe. I tried a few out-patient recovery programs, but they didn't work for me, either.

I don't want to slam recovery programs too hard; after all, without a recovery program, I would not be clean today. I cannot stress enough that the cure for addiction lies within each addict. It is up to the individual, and that individual will only be ready for the help a program can provide when he or she is ready, and not a moment before.

In my early recovery, I tried going back to work on days when I wasn't getting high, which proved to be a nightmare. Even though I wasn't high at work, the drugs were still rampant in my system and irrational thinking still dominated my mind, not to mention the generally shitty attitude I had from withdrawal.

I'd go into work ranting and raving about everything that was wrong, turn the place upside down and then not show up for a week, because I was back on crack. In hindsight, I don't know how my partner, Rich, put up with me.

As for my employees, if they didn't work for me pre-addiction, I didn't even know their names and couldn't bother with them. Rich and my manager, Clare, had just the right combination of patience, wisdom and common sense to let me rant and ignore what I said, while staying out of my way in order to avoid a major confrontation. I thank them for that.

Sometimes the hardest thing to do is to do nothing, and in that wisdom, they preserved the peace and kept Rachel's running. I don't know how they put up with me. I don't know that I would have had the strength to do the same had the shoe been on the other foot. Then on August 3, 2009, I went to jail.

Chapter Twenty

Jail

My stint in jail was brief...very brief. My sentence was 30 days. Well, it was actually 90 days. I got three 30-day sentences, but through some good lawyering, I was able to serve them concurrently and not consecutively. Either way, it was long enough to make me sure I never wanted to go back. It's a different state of existence, being cut off from the outside world, in a dank, dirty castle of steel and concrete—a place where you're in a perpetual state of mental submission and boredom is the order.

Think of the time it takes you to read a page of this book. Now, picture the rest of this book filled with blank pages. You stare at one blank page for the same amount of time it would take you to read it, flip the page and move on to the next for the same amount of time, then repeat the process for the time it takes to read 300 pages. Then, imagine doing this day after day and you will begin to have an idea of how slowly time passes in jail.

Jail is a place no one wants to be. You don't want to be an inmate and from what I could tell, many of the officers weren't too fond of their jobs there, either. Like with any group of people, most of the officers were fine and went about their tasks day after day and really didn't seem to give a shit about us either way. However, a few of the officers must have been abused as children and spent way more energy than necessary being pricks.

One of the lessons I learned quickly was to keep my head down and my mouth shut. It takes so much more effort to be an asshole than a normal person. My first week out of "72," meaning the first 72 hours you're in jail and confined to your cell for all but one hour a day for recreation, the 12 other guys on my cell block and I were walking single file along the right-hand side of the hallway as ordered, back from our hour of outdoor recreation. I asked one of the officers escorting us, "Excuse me, officer, but do you know what time the Giants game is on?" He gave me a shove and said, "What the fuck do you care? Shut the fuck up."

Now tell me it wouldn't have been easier to say, "I don't know," or "It's the four o'clock game and didn't start yet," or even ignore me and say nothing. Can you imagine asking a guy at a bar, as you walk in off the street, the same question and getting that reaction? It may sound trivial, but it's all part of the game of letting you know who the boss is and reducing you from feeling like a human being to feeling like a submissive identification number in an orange jumpsuit.

On the bright side, my time in jail was not as bad as they make it out to be in the movies, with gangs, and people getting shanked, raped and beaten senseless by the guards. At least my cell block wasn't like that, but it did suck. Even though Nassau County is a maximum security jail, I was not housed with rapists, murderers or violent criminals. However, I was housed in the same facility, with the same rules.

At 9 a.m. on a beautiful August morning, I went to criminal court in Mineola, NY, wearing a suit and tie, trying to look my best for sentencing. Even though I thought I looked good, I'm sure I looked every bit the dressed-up strung-out crackhead I was. Despite being clean since June, I had started on a binge a few days before sentencing and had taken my last hit in my friend's car parked across the street and walked straight into court.

I waited my turn to be reprimanded and sentenced for my crimes in Judge Kase's courtroom. The judge was, in my opinion, a fair and intelligent man. Through my many court appearances over the previous few months, I had witnessed him dole out justice from the bench with what I perceived as genuine concern and compassion, actually expressing his personal feelings and giving explanation to why he was sentencing the way he did. I had seen him give out both harsh and light sentences. I had even seen him disbar a lawyer and forbid him from applying for a license to practice law again for seven years.

My most serious crime was felony possession of a controlled substance. It was a B felony, which is up there in the alphabet of felonies and is considered a serious crime. New York State law aside, it was serious to me for two reasons: one, because it was fucking serious, and two, if I got convicted of a felony, I risked losing my liquor license, and what good is a restaurant with no liquor license? Oh yeah, and, if I went to trial and lost, that B felony came with three to five years in an upstate prison.

I had other charges, too. These included driving while under the influence, driving with a suspended license, aggravated unlicensed driving and a few other cases in district court for misdemeanor drug possession and some traffic violations that I was to be sentenced for later. Fortunately for me, after several months of hearings and considerable legal expenses, my lawyer was able to plea bargain my B felony charge down to a misdemeanor, which got me the 30 days in jail and three years of probation.

Although my crimes also came with a six-month motor vehicle suspension, Judge Kase took it a little further. He revoked my license for three years, citing first that since I had demonstrated that not only was I willing to drive under the influence of drugs, I was also willing to drive with a suspended license. Secondly, he went on to say that he did not want to share the road with someone like me, nor did he feel comfortable with me driving on the same roads as his kids and grandkids. Could you blame him?

As per his direction, I was to go to jail, come out and get help for my addiction. He went on to tell me that if I got caught driving without a license at any time during my three-year probation, whether I was high or not, he would put me back in jail.

OVERCOOKED

According to the rules of probation, you're not allowed to consume alcohol, or be in a bar or anywhere alcohol is served. Since Rachel's has a bar, technically I would not be allowed in my own business for three years. My attorney pointed out to the judge that I owned a restaurant and held a liquor license, and this would be detrimental to my livelihood. Judge Kase struck out the whole section concerning alcohol from my probation. I was too pissed off at that time about not being allowed to drive for three years while on probation to realize the judge had doled out his justice wisely, leaving the door wide open for my recovery.

My sentence was a fork in the road, with options for me to choose my own path. At this point, I was still too blind to see the path to hell on which I was traveling. I had been arrested five times in a little over a year and had a serious drug addiction that had me facing a maximum of five years in prison. I walked with 30 days, three years of probation and mandatory drug rehabilitation. It was a second chance and a new lease on life. All the tools I needed to get back on track were handed to me on a silver platter with the added incentive that if I fuck up, I go back to jail.

If you have never experienced the all-consuming power of addiction, what seems like a simple choice to most, is not that simple to an addict. The proof is in our jails that are full of people like me who were sentenced by judges like Kase. Unfortunately, many of them didn't eat off the silver platter that had been handed to them and went right back into the abyss. I got off with a light sentence—a sentence designed to give me a taste of the life I would have if I stayed on drugs, and an open door to recovery. I just had to want it.

Even now as a passenger in a car, I'm uncomfortable riding past areas where I used to buy drugs. I'm not even talking about the actual spot, just the main road I used to turn off of. I hadn't been to court since Judge Kase sentenced me, but recently had to return to district court. I was going to small claims court over a dispute at Rachel's. Anyway, going back through "the old neighborhood" gave me the heebie jeebies. The Nassau County District Court is located in Hempstead, two blocks east from one of the most notorious drug strips on Long Island, Terrace Ave.

As I was approaching the courthouse, we passed the golden arches across the street and I felt sick to my stomach. I had been to this courthouse many times and on more than one occasion had stopped into McDonald's in the morning before court, bought an Egg McMuffin, walked around the corner, threw out the sandwich and took a hit of crack. Then I put my pipe, lighter and crack into the McDonald's bag, walked to the courthouse and tossed it behind the garbage can right outside the door. I would wait in line to get through the metal detector, go to court, my lawyer would adjourn my case for another month and on my way out of the courthouse I'd simply grab my bag from behind the garbage and go back to getting high. Looking back now it's hard to believe what I had let myself come to.

Unlike movie courtrooms, Nassau County courtrooms are not lavishly decorated, trimmed in mahogany with large windows overlooking a courtyard. They're about as inviting and well-appointed as most motor vehicle offices, but compared to the basement of the courthouse, the courtroom was like a suite at the Waldorf Astoria.

Immediately after Judge Kase sentenced me, I was handcuffed in the courtroom by the correction officers standing behind me and brought down to the basement. The social graces these officers used while in the presence of the judges and lawyers all but disappeared. It was now "Shut the fuck up scumbag, and don't talk unless spoken to." I was immediately strip-searched, told to squat down and spread 'em. They took my belongings, put them into an envelope, sealed it and then I signed my name over the seal.

I was paraded into the hall and waited to be handcuffed to another inmate. I was now officially no longer a person: I was inmate number NC-09-76990755. We were handcuffed right arm to right arm. My right arm was along my right side, and the other inmate's right arm was across the front of his body attached to mine. We were then led to a holding cell filled with everyone else waiting for transportation to the jail. The cross-arm handcuffing is designed to make it more difficult to cause trouble and is also much more uncomfortable for the guy who is cross-armed.

My new partner must have had some prior experience with the court system, because as we entered the holding cell he made a quick spinning move and came around my back, and now I was the one whose arm was across his body. We waited that way for an hour or so, assimilating into our new environment in handcuffs, then off to a bus with about 10 other inmates and four guards for transport to jail. My man motioned politely for me to get on the bus ahead of him and I went up the steps first, got a front row seat, with my new buddy sitting in the seat right behind me. Now my handcuffed arm was up over my shoulder into the seat behind me. I turned around to look at him and he gave me a little smirk. This guy was good.

The rest of the 15-minute ride from the courthouse to jail was uneventful, which kind of goes without saying, as five pairs of handcuffed inmates, who were forbidden from speech, were escorted by four armed guards. The bus pulled into the lot at the Nassau County Jail and we disembarked under armed guard. We walked across the parking lot into the jail and began to get processed with fingerprints, picture ID, pin number for phone calls, and uniforms. After each step of the process, I would be put back into a cell until it was time for the next step. Nothing moves fast in jail. This is where I first experienced two new things unique to being in jail. The first is what I call jail talk. It could be described as sort of an English accent spoken with a rhythmic musical swagger. Like most accents, the longer you're around them, the more you start to pronounce words the way the locals do.

Even though the inmates were all from different ethnicities and walks of life, we somehow assimilated the jail lingo into our everyday conversations. The second thing is the smell—or should I say the stench—of jail. Twenty years from now you can blindfold me and pass that smell under my nose and I'll know it in a second. It's a festering smell of food, sweat, excrement and disinfectant steeped over time in a dank, dark, concrete dungeon. The air is a little thicker than outside and you can almost taste it on your tongue.

We were given baloney on white bread and half a pint of milk. An argument ensued between a couple of inmates over whether the baloney was made with turkey or beef, which led to a fist fight. A couple of guys broke it up before the guards came. I inched my way to the back of the cell, head down looking at the ground. I wasn't looking anyone in the eye. I figured the best way to avoid trouble in jail is to avoid it, so right then and there, I made that my policy.

It was going on two in the afternoon and I was crashing hard from being up for a few days, and I hadn't eaten in just as long. I took a bite of my whatever on white bread, opened the milk and took a big swig. Before I could actually taste it, I felt the curdled lumps going down my throat. Welcome to Nassau County Jail, Asshole.

Some inmates have jobs. The non-violent ones serving longer sentences are the primary workforce in the Nassau County Correction Facility. Some of the jobs include cooking, laundry, and distribution of commissary, which is the equivalent to the jail's general store, and "Tier man," which we'll get into later.

Our next step was uniforms, which involved another strip search. What did they think I could have picked up in the last three hours, locked in a cell and under guard? I'll never know, but they seemed determined to find it. They took our clothes and shoes and made us sign off on them. An inmate took my measurements and shoe size, and sent it off while I got strip-searched.

I happened to know the inmate who brought me my new clothes. Lucky me. That statement was not a bit sarcastic. Pauly gave me extra t-shirts and socks plus a brand new, not used, pair of shoes, which was really a pair of Kung Fu slippers. The extra t-shirts and socks later proved invaluable when doing laundry, as these were my only clothes and at least I could wear a t-shirt while I washed my orange dress clothes. I also got my cup, toothbrush, soap, toothpaste and towel. Unlike a cup or toothbrush at home, these were valuable commodities, as I was told I would only receive one of each. I thanked him and then it was off to medical.

The same dozen of us who had been going through the system together all morning were escorted unhandcuffed in our new bright orange duds, walking single file along the right side of the hallway hugging the wall. No talking was allowed. "Medical" consisted of a brief physical with voluntary blood work, AIDS and tuberculosis tests, among others, and a psychological exam. The psychological part was brief. I was brought into a small office with someone I assume was a psychologist, and I was asked a few questions, predominantly revolving around the issues of wanting to hurt anyone or the desire to kill myself. Apparently, I passed the test and was now ready for General Population.

It takes 72 hours to determine the results of the tuberculosis test; inmates are isolated in individual cells to await the test results. This time period is referred to by inmates and guards as… you guessed it, "72." My cell was in B block, a row of about 15 cells all painted puke green. My recollection is that if it wasn't raw concrete or stainless steel, it was puke green. Our cells were appointed with a one-piece stainless sink/toilet combo, shelf, bed and mattress. In front of our cells, running parallel was our common area, an 8-foot-wide walkway with two phones, a shower and a couple of stainless steel picnic tables on one end and a television on the other. The cells and common area were encased by a set of bars. On the other side of the bars was a second walkway about 5 feet wide for the guards to walk through and observe us, which they did every 15 minutes. Then there was the cinder-block exterior wall with a few small barred windows along the ceiling that we were able to see bits of sky through.

The worst part of jail for me was "72." If you refused to get the tuberculosis test or give blood, they kept you in 72 indefinitely, as was the case with the gentleman in the first cell on the block, A cell. A-Cell was his nickname, as well as the name of his domicile. Until we were cleared for general population, we were let out of our cells individually for an hour a day. We woke at 5:30 a.m. to wait to be served breakfast by the Tier Man, who was chosen by the guards. I don't know the criteria for the job, or how the guards decided on who the Tier Man was, but it was usually a person with seniority regarding how much time he would be spending in jail.

The Tier Man had power, because he regulated who got what food. There was usually an extra slice of bread or fruit, or sometimes even a whole tray of food that could be exchanged or traded for other items. If you wanted to trade something from another inmate you had to go through him—he was the only one with access to the other prisoners.

Since there is no currency in jail, you had to trade for something or owe someone a favor if you wanted something. A-Cell had refused his blood test and was serving his entire sentence in 72. He had everything: Vicodin, coke, weed, and cigarettes. He even had a pillow. Pillows were officially nonexistent in jail. If you had one and got transferred to a different block, they took it away. You couldn't requisition one or buy one from the commissary. I have no idea how they got there, they just did. I only saw one other pillow during my stay and it got taken away when we transferred blocks.

When my fellow inmates' and my first 72 hours had passed, we did not move out of B block, but our restrictions were eased and we were allowed to roam around the common area for most of the day. We were not allowed into each other's cells. As I adjusted to jail life, I was becoming a little more outspoken and was slowly giving up on my policy of isolationism.

B block needed some kind of repair, so for a few days we were moved to another building into the "open dorms." It was a big open room that resembled a gymnasium with cots and picnic tables lined up for meals and socializing. It was like Club Med to us. I learned here just how valuable trivial things become to people when they have nothing. Extra slices of bread, an apple, or packet of drink mix were the most valuable possessions the majority of inmates would ever have and were traded like commodities on the stock exchange.

There was an inmate nicknamed "Old Man." Why? Because that's what he was: a frail, white-haired gentleman in his late 70s who weighed no more than 130 pounds. He arrived on our block about a week or so after I did. One afternoon, I was sitting having lunch at the tables in the open dorm with the old man and two young kids. Tier Man had a few extra slices of bread and he gave me and one of the kids at our table an extra slice. As we were finishing our lunch, the old man asked the kid if he could have his extra slice of bread, if he wasn't going to eat it. The kid just smiled and passed over the bread. As soon as the old man took a bite this punk says, "Now you owe me, old man." I was furious. Really? Over a piece of bread you didn't want anyway? What a piece of shit. In my rage, I threw my slice of bread at this scumbag and told him, "The old man owes you nothing!"

I didn't notice at the time, but that incident gave me the respect of the other inmates and I suddenly developed my "crew" of guys who would congregate together. It makes me sick to even think about that now, but that's how petty things are in jail. Me and my crew talked all day about everything there was to talk about. We had nothing else to do. I guess my being a restaurant owner and not just your average skell also elevated my stature. Rah fucking rah.

One afternoon at lunch I was bitching about the food rather loudly. To say the food in jail sucks is an understatement. According to the Association of Correctional Food Service Affiliates, as of Sept 2016, jails can feed prisoners for as little as $1.20 per day. Cabbage, for example, is a cheap vegetable but not cheap enough for jail. Our coleslaw consisted of about 33 percent shredded cabbage and 66 percent of some kind of thin squiggly pasta to cut the cabbage with, a dash of mayo and a shredded carrot here and there. Fish sandwich day, a meal I actually looked forward to, I can best describe as a shaved piece of fish about the thickness of a sheet of newspaper, breaded, fried, and served on a bun. The fruits they served were the smallest apples, oranges, peaches and pears I'd ever seen, about the size of apricots. Oh, and the coffee? I'm not sure what that hot brown liquid was. According to one of my fellow inmates nicknamed Roadblock, it was chicory. I have no idea, but it was definitely not coffee.

I was bitching about the food rather vocally, saying that a box of salt and pepper packets costs about $4 for 2,000 packages and I'm sure the jail can find something for half that price. For some reason, this was very interesting to the other inmates as I started talking about the cost of food service in jail. This prompted the guards to escort me out of the room and into a private area and pretty much accuse me of trying to organize a riot among the inmates.

I found out they had been keeping an eye on me since the bread incident with the Old Man. Believe me, it was not a friendly conversation—let's leave it at that. So much for freedom of speech. I quickly readapted my policy of isolationism for the rest of my stay.

OVERCOOKED

Photos

Ivan Sayles

January, 1986. Me waiting on Uncle Archie and Aunt Millie at the Culinary Institute of America.

Opening of Rachel's. 1996.

When your friend, Mark, shows up to your "Kids-Eat-Free" promo with a fake I.D. Rachel's Waterside Grill.

Me, Rich, an Mike at the Bayou Rum Distillery

Ivan Sayles

Delivering by boat from Rachel's.

With Dalton, Zoie, and Amanda. Using free child labor in our ads.

That time the sprinkler system went off on opening night at NAWLINS, (now known as TROPIX ON THE BAYOU).

Several times a year, trucks would run into the beautiful and remarkably strong stone bridges that Robert Moses built. Sometimes they make it through. Sometimes they don't.

Free roll of toilet paper with every family meal promotion during COVID-19 pandemic.

Sampling the local charcuterie cheeses and wine in Marseille, France.

Me and Rich
visiting the
Cuban Culinary
Federation.

David Sattanino
(9/22/94 - 1/9/2017)

Veronica Birk
(1/7/92 - 12/8/17)

Butchering Long Island's freshest tuna. Caught in the Canyons, 180 miles offshore, by the wickedest anglers I know: Mike, Jimmy and Billy.

Alligator hunting in Lacassine, Louisiana with my partner, Rich.

RACHEL'S and TROPIX ON THE BAYOU (formerly NAWLINS)

Getting ready to take the plunge for the March of Dimes Polar Bear Swim Super Bowl Sunday. Long Beach, Long Island. February 2, 2020

Cooking demo for kids with Down's Syndrome

Knifed by the Great Throwdini at Tropix on the Bayou (formerly Nawlins)

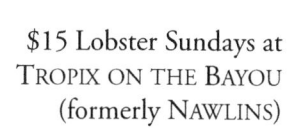

$15 Lobster Sundays at Tropix on the Bayou (formerly Nawlins)

Ivan Sayles

Before you judge me, read Chapter 37, titled: "Me, Jen, and Gov. Andrew Cuomo."

Cheffing up some crab cakes for charity.

Salmon for the masses at
the Nassau County Bar
Association.

Table-side fresh mozzarella
at RACHEL'S WATERSIDE
GRILL.

Ivan Sayles

Charity tasting event

Shooting flaming arrows into Woodcleft Canal at our company picnic. Freeport - Nautical Mile. Oct. 14, 2019.

Ivan Sayles

Chapter Twenty-one

What a Cloud Smells Like

I believe vacations are the main reason I've been placed here on Earth. More than once I've thought to myself while basking in the sun, sipping on my fruity, girly tropical cocktail, holding the stem of the glass in proper form, between my index finger and thumb, pinkie out, Why do I work? I'm so much better at this.

One of my favorite places to go in the United States is the Florida Keys, particularly Key West. A three and a half-hour drive from Miami along Route 1, otherwise known as the Overseas Highway, it's a 127-mile stretch from Key Largo to Key West. A name has never been so well suited to a road. It's mostly one lane in each direction, which can be best enjoyed by renting a car with a retractable roof.

I absolutely love driving the route, feeling the sun warming my skin under a cloudless blue sky. Its landscape is lined with green mangroves creeping toward the white concrete, trying to engulf the road with their finger-like roots. The mangroves are so overbearing in some areas it feels like you're driving through a tunnel. Suddenly, land ends and you find yourself in open air over the water, driving across one of the many bridges with their spectacular ocean views.

My favorite span is the 6.79 miles connecting Knights Key to Little Duck Key, appropriately named the Seven Mile Bridge. The view is spectacular: the Gulf of Mexico is on the southern side, with its flat, shimmering turquoise-green water, and the

Florida Strait is on the other. Cuba lies only 80 miles to the south and sometimes I think if I look hard enough, I'll actually see it.

I was 34 when I went skydiving for the first time. It was the annual Key West trip from Jackie Reilly's, an Irish pub owned by two guys named Sean—Sean R. and Sean H. Sean R. was a friend of mine for many years, since Eddie, Rich and I, along with the rest of the crew at Jones Beach, used to visit him behind the stick (the beer tap) at The Wantagh Inn in the mid-'80s.

The vacation crew consisted of New York City and Nassau County cops and firemen, bartenders, cooks, myself and Sean. We took the first morning flight out of JFK to Miami. Several of the guys brought their suitcases to the bar the night before and took a cab straight from Jackie's to the airport. Once in Florida, we rented a couple of cars, stopped for beer and began our journey to Key West.

One of the first things I notice when out of my native Long Island is how much friendlier everyone is to each other than back at home. Being from New York, it is especially gratifying to be able to enjoy the greetings of complete strangers. As the story goes, two tourists are lost in Manhattan and they stop a cab driver to ask for directions. One tourist asks, "Excuse me sir, would you mind telling me how to get to Central Park—or should I just go fuck myself?" Well, it's not really that bad, but we New Yorkers can be a rude bunch.

I truly grasped this, on one particular vacation, leaving my hotel room early one morning while strolling to a breakfast buffet. A complete stranger walking in the opposite direction greeted me with a smile and a "good morning." I turned my head from left to right, looking to see who he was talking to. I was so caught off guard that he practically walked past me before I realized he was talking to me, and I returned the pleasantry.

Kidding aside, I could use a little work on my people skills, but being a victim of my environment, this strange greeting definitely caught me off guard. If you live in NYC or its suburbs, try saying good morning to everyone who passes you one day. I do it now and again for shits and giggles. My tally is one-third will look at you like you're nuts, one-third will ignore you, and one-third will actually respond in kind and say good morning. I've received a few comments posted on Yelp by unhappy customers who didn't like the way I spoke to them. It's not that I don't want to make my customers happy. I do. I would do anything for them. It's just that sometimes I forget to push my people-person button when I wake up.

By the time our group got to Sugarloaf Key, we had put a big dent in the beer and our bladders were screaming. We pulled into Mangrove Mama's, the traditional stop for our Key West adventures. The view from above as our cars pulled into the lot must have been comical. Tires came to an abrupt dusty stop, skidding into the parking lot dotted with crunchy clam shells.

All twelve doors of three cars burst open simultaneously as we ran across the lot, into the building and straight past the hostess to the bathroom. Returning one by one, the hostess with her friendly Floridian smile sat us down for lunch. Some of us were drunk, some had just woken up, and all three drivers were stressed out. Trying to order lunch was a nightmare; no one could decide what he wanted. Guys kept changing their minds after someone ordered something that sounded better than what they'd ordered. It took the poor waitress forever to get it straight.

With the order finally in, we drew straws for roommates while we waited for our meal to arrive. This was a tradition on all Jackie Reilly trips. I ended up being roomed with a New York City fireman named Gill, someone I had never met before this trip. By the time lunch arrived, everyone had shaken hands and agreed on the hotel arrangements. We ate, picked up some more beer and began the final half-hour of our drive to Key West. I happened to notice a road sign that said "Skydiving." Hmm… that looks like fun.

We arrived at our traditional spot, the Southernmost Hotel in the United States, which is not only a true statement, but also the hotel's name. We checked in and went to our rooms to freshen up and agreed to meet later at the pool bar, which served breakfast, lunch and dinner. We began arriving in pairs at the bar. What a sight we were, a bunch of young men with New York accents, wearing loud shirts and screaming in even louder voices.

Our red faces were lined with white stripes on each side of our temples, and the smell of suntan lotion and cheap cologne engulfed our group. The few of us who got to our rendezvous point were anxiously awaiting the arrival of the last two guys, so we could go out on the town. We were an unstoppable group of young men in the best shape of our lives, ready to eat, drink and fuck everything there was in Key West. It must have been horrifying to the other guests.

Our pockets filled with cash, we set off down Duval St. to see what damage we could do. We chose a nice restaurant. I don't recall the name. Businesses come and go so quickly down there my guess is that it's probably been a few different places since my last visit. We had a great meal and some good wine. We might lack manners and social graces, but we sure have eating and drinking in excess down to a science.

Knowing that this was the last we would all be together that night, we agreed to meet at 10 a.m. the next day at the pool bar at our hotel before we broke up into smaller groups and headed out. Duval St. is the main drag on Key West. It runs 1.2 miles north-south from the Gulf of Mexico to the Atlantic Ocean. It's the ultimate tourist strip with hotels, restaurants, shops, bars, strip clubs, gay clubs, even clothing-optional clubs, and plenty of ATMs. The gracious city of Key West closes its bars at 4 a.m. and even allows you to bring your alcoholic beverage into the street with you when leaving an establishment. This is not a town for amateurs.

Without boring you with the gory details of my night (mostly because I don't remember), suffice it to say I was too drunk to walk back to the hotel. It was approaching 3 a.m. and I had been drinking since the plane landed that morning. The streets were still crowded with pedestrians and I caught a ride in one of the many bicycle rickshaws cruising up and down Duval. I passed a few of the guys on the way back to the hotel. We exchanged obscenities at each other as my man pedaled on.

When I got back to the room, my roommate Gill wasn't back yet. God bless that guy, I thought, and the last thing I remember before nodding off was counting the ink stamps on my hands from all the clubs I had been to: six, as I recall. Not too shabby for my first night in Key West.

I woke up the next morning at the crack of 10:00 a.m. Gill was not there and his bed was made. Cool, I thought. At least one of us got laid last night. I tried to put together what I did the night before but wasn't having any luck. Head pounding, I hopped in the shower, got dressed and went to the pool bar. As guys started trickling down from their rooms for breakfast, the stories from the night before were recounted and repeated and expanded on as each guy joined the table.

One of the guys in particular had obviously just rolled out of bed and come straight downstairs, neglecting even to look in the mirror. His hair was sticking straight up and a stamp from one of the clubs was smack in the middle of his forehead where a bouncer had put it the night before. We were down two men at breakfast: my roommate and Sean.

By the time Sean came down to join us, some of us were already on our second Bloody Mary, and we were speculating about which girl Gill had gone home with. As he approached our table, Sean announced to the group in his Irish brogue, "Well, boys, it looks like it's gonna be $100.00 a man for Gill's bail.

Ends up Gill did not get laid but instead got shot down by a girl and stormed out of a bar. To get back at her and prove what a man he was, he broke the side-view mirrors of 10 cars parked along the road. We men can be such idiots.

Sean collected our money and drove to the county jail to pick Gill up. We all agreed to meet up for lunch at the Hog's Breath Saloon, a Key West icon. We ordered beers and opened our menus. As soon as our waitress came over to take our order, one of the guys immediately took control. After the fiasco of placing our lunch order on the road, he was having no part of it. He screamed out, "We'll have eleven cheeseburgers and a chicken sandwich!" That was good enough for me. We all looked at each other, nodded, closed our menus, and went back to our beers. What was next on my agenda that day? Skydiving!

I can't even begin to describe the thrill of jumping out of a plane. I don't think the English language has adjectives appropriate for the story. Maybe it does, but I certainly don't possess them. All I can say is everyone should do it at least once. Since my first jump, I've gone three more times. None of that static-line bullshit either: all freefall.

I called to get some information about skydiving and found out there are two kinds of jumps first-timers can do. The first is called a "static line jump" and the second is a "tandem jump." The static line jump is the kind you see in World War II movies, where the soldiers attach their chute to a static line or a wire on the plane that causes the parachute to deploy upon exiting the plane. This type of jump takes place at an altitude of around 3,000 feet.

The disadvantage of the static line jump is in the limited time you free fall, which is the time from when you jump out of the plane and plummet to the earth at 130 miles per hour until your chute opens. For the first-time jumper, the advantage to the static line jump is that you can exit the plane alone. The second type, the tandem jump, takes place three miles above the earth. In this case, you and your instructor, who is strapped to your back, roll out of the plane together, free fall for about 25 seconds, pull the chute at 4,500 feet and drift down to earth.

Me being me, I asked the woman on the phone if there was any way possible I could do the free fall jump by myself without the burden of having someone strapped to my back. She was very polite and told me I could do whatever I wanted. She suggested as a first timer, I didn't even have to use a parachute. But if I wanted to dive with them and live to do it a second time, I would have to do it their way, and their way was tandem. There's nothing I love more than sarcasm, especially when someone is throwing it back in my face. I explained the situation to the group and several of us agreed to go, but in the end it was just Johnny and me. The rest of the women stayed at the bar.

Now, I'm no homophobe, but I'm also not accustomed to a grown man being strapped to my back. However, in this situation, I have to say that having a grown man harnessed tightly against my back in no way diminished the thrill of jumping from a plane and falling to the earth at 130 miles per hour. Plus, he's a great guy to have right there in a pinch, like say, if I forget to pull the rip cord.

Johnny and I drove to Skydive Key West, which by the way is not located in Key West at all, but 20 miles away in Sugarloaf Key. Our instructor gave us a 30-minute crash course in the fine art of falling to the ground, including stories of his most memorable jumps, pictures of other people skydiving and some words of wisdom. "Don't look down during the free fall; stare out at the horizon and enjoy the view. You'll have plenty of time to look down once the chute opens, plus you can't really breathe with the wind rushing directly into your face." Oh yeah: "For an additional $175 you can buy the video of your jump," which of course we both did.

After our skydiving lesson, we walked down the runway, put on our jumpsuits and helmets, strapped on our instructors and their parachutes and readied ourselves to board the plane. It couldn't have been a more perfect day: 85 degrees, sunny and a deep blue sky with a few puffy white clouds drifting in the gentle breeze. It was here that I met the cameraman who was going to video the jump, and as Gomer Pyle used to say, "Well…Surprise! Surprise! Surprise!" It was the same wise-ass woman I had spoken to on the phone earlier. This was getting better by the minute. Strapped to the top of her helmet was a monstrosity of a camera that had to weigh more than her head. Mind you, this was pre–Selfie Stick/Go Pro. She was recording with a VHS camera.

They pointed to our plane on the runway, a single-engine, top-winged plane whose shiny white paint and bright red pin-striping had long since given in to the forces of Mother Nature and were now faded, grayish, orangey and dull. As we approached the aircraft, we met the pilot, shook hands and climbed in. OMG! What a piece of shit this thing was. The upholstery from the ceiling had come unglued and was hanging down on me like it did in my 1973 Olds Omega (Buccaneer red with a Rocket 350, if you recall).

The seats of the plane had been removed except for the pilot's, and there was an ashtray in the armrest that was still attached to the hull of the plane, in case you want a last cigarette before your plummet to earth. They haven't allowed smoking on planes since the '80s, so I figured this plane is at least 30 years old, but I wasn't going to ask, for fear I was wrong and it might be older. We climbed in and sat on the floor facing each other with knees to our chests, and the instructor closed the door.

Instantly, it felt like the temperature rose 20 degrees as the sun baked down on the fuselage. My heart was racing with excitement and sweat began dripping down my face. The pilot started cranking up the engine. Dunnuna, nunana, nunana.... Again Dunnuna, nunana, nunana. Was this for real or were they just fucking with me? Dunnuna, nunana, nunana, and finally Vrooom! The engine roared to life, and after letting her warm up for a few minutes, down the runway we taxied westward to take off.

As we started our noisy climb to our jumping altitude, somewhere around three miles up in the air, the plane banked left out over the Atlantic Ocean. The stench of gasoline and oil from takeoff was replaced by the smell of fresh warm salty sea air blowing into the cabin. The view of the Florida Keys from the air was nothing short of spectacular. Again, we were circa pre–Google Earth, so not too much in the way of aerial photography was available to the public, and seeing things like this was truly amazing.

As far as I could see, there were rows of islands dotting the sea of turquoise green water, homes and building developments carved out of the lush green mangroves. The sands cascading away from the islands caused the shades of ocean to change from whitish aqua green in the shallows to a bluish green as the waters got deeper. We watched traffic slowly cruise from island to island over the bridges of the Overseas Highway.

Had I not been on the plane for the sole purpose of jumping out of it, I would have been content to have paid just for the view spanning Key West to Miami. It was truly magnificent, and then as we banked left again and headed east I could see Cuba out in the distance. As we approached our drop zone, a few last instructions were shouted above the roar of the plane's engine and it was time to jump.

When the instructor popped open the side door of the plane, I was hit by a wall of hot air and the noise of the engine jumped from loud to deafening. As if all this wasn't stimulating enough, I was shocked when the woman who was going to take my video climbed out of the plane onto the supporting bar of the wing and sat on it in order to get the shot of me falling out of the plane. In retrospect, I guess, this was really the only way to get such a shot, but with all that was going on, I really didn't think it through.

With my instructor behind me, we swung our legs out the open door. My ass in the plane, my feet dangling three miles high, we got the green light. I don't remember actually seeing a green light, but I'm sure it was there somewhere. My instructor and I rocked forward together, leaning slightly out of the plane like I was taught. "Yabba" we shouted together, rocked backward into the plane, "Dabba" we hollered. This was it! Rocking forward again and rolling and out of the safety of the plane into the open air, we screamed,"Doooooo!"

OVERCOOKED

I thought I would lose my stomach like when plunging down on a roller coaster, but it didn't happen. Flipping over, as we plummeted toward the ground, I saw the bottom of the plane for a brief second and then it was gone as we were twisted and turned toward the ground again. After a few brief glimpses of Earth and sky, then Earth and sky, my instructor aided me in fanning out our legs and arms until we established a sort of spread eagle belly flop position, stabilizing our spin into controlled motion.

Even through the helmet, the roar of tearing through the air at 130 miles an hour was tremendous. I never thought falling would be so loud. Staring down at the ground beneath me, I found it very difficult to breathe with the wind rushing into my face. Then my instructor's words popped back into my head, "Don't look down, look out at the horizon and enjoy the freefall; you'll have plenty of time to look down when the chute opens."

As I looked out onto the horizon, my lungs filled with air and my breathing was instantly restored to normal and for the first time, I noticed there was a third person falling to the ground. I was staring right into the face of the camera woman who had positioned herself in the same spread eagle pose about five feet directly in front of my face. This was absolutely fantastic. We folded in our left arms and we began to spin left, straightened it out and we stabilized, vice versa for the right side. Could it have been 30 seconds already?

My altimeter said we were fast approaching 4,500 feet and it was time to pull the cord. My instructor tapped my leg, and as instructed to do when I felt him do that, I yanked on the rip cord with all my might. The chute popped out and flew open. It was like being torn out of my shoes by my shoulder straps. My feet shot straight up in front of me in recoil from the sudden reduction in speed. I heard the wind catch the chute with a whoosh.

Instantly, we went from racing at 130 miles an hour to drifting gently at 20 miles an hour. The woman in front of me seemed to vanish before my eyes. I looked down and saw a tiny speck of what had once been the person in front of me. She was headed down ahead of us to video our landing. Then what seemed like miles beneath me, I saw the vibrant reds and yellows of her canopy unfold, resembling time-lapse photography of a blooming flower. What was mere seconds ago a roaring, noisy, chaotic free fall was instantly a silent, smooth drift. The only noise in the sky was the wind gently rippling through the parachute.

It was now time to look down and it was beautiful. Surprisingly, the view from 16,000 feet to 4,500 feet hadn't changed that much. Below us and off to the side, I noticed a puffy white cumulus cloud and asked my instructor if we could steer into it and he obliged. Together we reigned in the toggle ropes on the left side of the parachute, dipping that corner of the chute down and redirected it to the left, which cascaded us into a gentle counterclockwise spiral downward toward the cloud.

As we descended closer toward the cloud, things started to change. I could feel short gusts of air pushing up at us, transcending our smooth glide into a slightly choppy coast. Just as we entered the cloud, the temperature dropped what felt like 15 degrees, the air became turbulent and we started bouncing around in our harnesses, caught up in the warm air meeting cooler air.

Then I noticed the most astonishing thing of all: the smell. It was the same musty smell that permeates your nostrils on a warm summer day moments before a thunder shower. Poof, it was over, and we were through the cloud with a splash of warm air in the face. We remained under its shadow for a few more seconds and then back out into the sunshine, silence and warm sea air once again. We approached the ground right on target, drifting to a stand-up landing, right next to the camera.

OVERCOOKED

Chapter Twenty-two

Maggots

My years at The Boardwalk Restaurant helped shape me into the man and restaurateur I am today. It's where I learned about kickbacks, scams and countless ways of cheating the boss. It's also where I learned organizational skills, management, how to plan events for thousands, and the fine art of kissing the boss's ass...and it's where I got most of my hands-on practical restaurant experience. The Culinary Institute of America gave me some great building blocks and general knowledge, but it was at the Boardwalk Restaurant where I learned the real life skills needed to succeed for 25 years at Rachel's.

In 1986 the corporate powers that be, along with the guidance of Mike A., decided to remodel the restaurant. I was 21 years old, sitting in a meeting with the architects, planners, construction people and restaurant mavens, all at least twice my age. I didn't know it yet, but this meeting would become a life-shaping moment for me. One of the big-shot consultants was going over plans for the kitchen, specifically the hot line, or as we called it, "hot side." He stated we were redesigning the cooking line from scratch and that the left side of the line would be designed to handle 70 percent of the business and the right side, 30 percent. That didn't make too much sense to me, so I raised my hand and asked a simple question. "If we're designing a line from scratch, why don't we redo it to handle 100 percent of the business?"

His response to me, ignoring my question was, "How many kitchens have you Designed?

"None," I said.

He said, "Well, then I stand on my reputation!" My blood was boiling.

Why did this 50-something-year-old man need to slam the door so hard on a 21-year-old kid? Embarrassed, I said nothing for the rest of the meeting. That day, I learned a couple of the most important lessons of my career, including the answer to my question of why a grown man would blow off kid, and in front of other people like that? Because he was an incompetent, egotistical jackass who needs to put other people down to make himself feel important. I'm now in my 50s, in his shoes, if you will, and have built and designed five restaurants. If I were asked a similar question, I would explain my reasons, number 1, because I would have legitimate ones for doing what I was doing, and number 2, because someone asked me a question in a meeting and deserves the respect of an answer.

Lesson Number 1:

Anyone who is asked a direct question and gives an indirect answer or avoids the question, is full of shit.

"Is the sun out?"

"Well, it rained yesterday."

"No, my question was, 'Is the sun out?'"

"I hear it's going to be quite chilly out today."

"Can you tell me if it's sunny out right now?" Honest, straightforward people give honest straightforward answers; bullshitters don't.

Lesson Number 2:

Never again have I let anyone slam the door like that on me. No matter how important or high level people think they are, we are all equal. We all put our pants on one leg at a time. Someone may have a higher position, make more money or have more responsibility than me, but as of that day, I realized that no one person is better than anyone else.

Lesson Number 3:
I have never again asked a question and accepted another question as an answer, or accepted an answer to a question I didn't ask. I've trained my management, when dealing with vendors, salesmen or contractors, to keep asking or changing the format of their question until the question is answered.

Upon our reopening of the "New Boardwalk Restaurant," we were sporting a redesigned ultra-efficient kitchen which, truth be told, was not really that different from the old one. We had a couple of under-counter freezers and refrigerators, a chargrill and newer versions of the same equipment we had before, in pretty much the same spot as before. Air-conditioning was added, which is always a plus in a commercial kitchen. It was also home to the cashier's booth, as well as the service bar—two features that I have not seen again together in a kitchen in a long time, although I'm sure they still exist.

I don't know whose idea it was to put the service bar in the kitchen. I'd like to think it was my friend, the consultant. What a fucking idiot. I suppose he and the other out-of-state restaurant consultants had no way of predicting the drinking habits of New York State Park Police, even though I'd like to blame them for not knowing.

Our service bar doubled as the unofficial, Official NY State Park Police Bar. Thirty years ago the State Park Police were a fun bunch of guys, mostly veterans of other police forces put out to pasture in the State Park Police system, waiting out their final few years until retirement and pension collection.

They'd park their cars on the loading dock and come up the stairs through the back of the kitchen, oblivious to what was going on in the restaurant at the time. Their timing was always impeccable, coming into the kitchen during the lunch or dinner rush…or they would just happen to be swinging by, empty plate in hand, as the last few orders of prime rib were being sliced and served at a wedding. After gorging themselves on free food, they made sure to pass by our service bar to top off their thermos with "coffee" before they went back out on patrol.

This meant that just as we were getting buried with lunch orders, Rosey, actually one of my favorite cops, would come over to the hot side, chewing on a piece of bacon he had just grabbed from under the heat lamp on the cold side, and ask the cook for a Reuben sandwich with extra lean pastrami, not too much sauerkraut, mozzarella instead of Swiss, and would we mind putting some mustard on it for him, too?

Stop the presses! Rosey ordered a sandwich! Everyone on the hot side would stop what they were doing to lend a hand in making this special sandwich for Rosey, lest they get pulled over for speeding on the way home. They could say they cooked lunch for cops at the Boardwalk in the hope of being sent on their way, ticketless.

One of my cooks, Eddie G., came to me one day and showed me an open container ticket he had gotten for drinking a beer in the parking lot of the theater at Jones Beach before a concert the night before. I asked him if he told the cop where he worked, and he said he did not. On the ticket, I saw the cop's name and told Ed to sit tight. The next time that cop came in, I mentioned the ticket to him. He immediately got in his cruiser and drove the 15 or so miles out to Captree, where Ed was working that day, to get the ticket back and apologize, mortified his free food and booze would be at risk.

While the sandwich of all sandwiches was being made for Rosey, he had just enough time to flirt with our head cashier, Wendy, a five-foot-eleven bombshell with curly blond hair and striking emerald green eyes. Her cubicle had one of those split doors that could have the top half open for easy transactions during the day, but could be closed to secure the office at night.

Inside was the cash register on a small desk surrounded by three sheetrock walls and a drop ceiling that consisted of fluorescent lighting and ceiling tiles with vent holes in them. Apparently during the final phases of construction, something had found its way above the cashier's booth and died up in the ceiling, where it had been festering.

Wendy had been complaining about a bad smell but no one could figure out what it was, until a day or two later, when maggots started falling out of the ceiling onto the cash register and into Wendy's hair. I don't know which scream was more bone chilling: the one when she realized maggots were falling down in her hair or the one a week later, when my future business partner Rich lobbed a handful of rice into her cubicle.

OVERCOOKED

Chapter Twenty-three

How to Become a Crack Addict in Two Easy Steps

Step 1: Disposable Income • **Step 2:** Time

It was the spring of 2005, the economy was healthy, I was making money, and Vic and I began building "spec" homes in Florida. Rachel's was doing well, practically running on autopilot, and I was getting a little bored with it. I was preoccupied, looking for a new challenge. I began drinking and sniffing cocaine five or six days a week. Unbeknownst to me at the time, I was becoming irritable, cranky and short tempered, self-centered, thinking of no one but myself, just looking to get my paycheck, go out and get high.

On a June weekend in 2006 after the Freeport Festival, I told Rich I didn't want to work anymore...I was retiring. I was 40 years old. I had a boat, a couple of rental homes, a house in Southampton, two hundred grand in the bank, and I was making plenty of money building and flipping houses in Florida. Rich and I spoke at length. I didn't feel I should collect a salary, as I wasn't putting in any hours, and he would have to hire another manager. Rich, believing I was just burnt out and needed a break, suggested I keep my salary and see how things panned out.

Knowing who I was, he figured I would get bored quickly and be back to work soon enough.

His theory was right; he just didn't factor in the drugs. It wasn't long before I started running into an old acquaintance of mine—the crack pipe—occasionally mixing the crack with angel dust and smoking them together. Smoking crack wasn't a new thing for me, but learning how to make it from powdered cocaine was.

I had smoked on and off for years, but my ability to get it, as well as my desire to do it, had been sporadic…until one day at a bar, when I ran into a friend, a woman I had known since high school and used to drink and sniff coke with in the bars. We drank and partied 'til closing time, then got a room. It was there that I learned to make crack from powder. She showed me how to mix the baking soda and coke, how to heat it in a spoon with a lighter, cool it and extract the crack. Later on she even taught me how to make crack in the microwave. Half-naked in the hotel room, we started to get high. I had smoked before, but it was never under these circumstances. She handed me the pipe and I took a hit. Maybe it was the quality of the stuff, maybe it was the fact that we made it ourselves, I don't know…but this was the hit that steered me into the abyss.

The smoke is not harsh like cigarettes or pot; it's actually a little sweet. Not too much happens on the inhale, but as you exhale, every worry, every pain and every care in the world flows out of your lungs along with the sweetness of the smoke. It's a feeling of relief and ecstasy at the same time. I handed her the pipe and she took a hit, then handed it back.

While I loaded it for my second hit, Leslie started unbuckling my pants and went down on me. As she took me in her mouth, I drew in on the glass pipe, while she simultaneously exhaled the warm smoke from her hit around my cock. The feeling of her hot, wet mouth sliding down me as I got hard combined with the euphoria of taking a hit was utterly amazing.

It was this combination of sex and drugs that would be my downfall over the next three years. I began hanging out with her and smoking more and more. I would stroll into Rachel's every now and then, being of no use to anyone. I'd bark a few orders at the waitstaff, bitch at Rich about everything I thought was wrong with Rachel's, grab some money and go back to what, at the time, was still a secret life. But hey, I was king. I wasn't working, I was getting high and getting my dick sucked, and the best thing of all, I was collecting a paycheck every week.

No one, least of all me, saw what was coming next. Within two months I was smoking crack every day. I had begun my downward spiral, forsaking friends, family and responsibility all for the want of a glass pipe and a tiny rock. I was introduced to new "friends." The circle of crack smokers in Bellmore was not that large and within a few months I was hanging out with the lot of them and had been introduced to all the local dealers.

The girls wanted to hang out with me because I shared my drugs with them, and the dealers wanted to do business with me because I bought a lot and paid cash. There's one more element in the equation that became crucial to my access to drugs and contributed tremendously to my addiction: the Automated Teller Machine.

The ATM is the single greatest asset to the drug trade. It's the only place you can get $300 in cash at 3:00 in the morning without stealing it. As Chris Rock used to say, "No one needs $300 at 3 o'clock in the morning for anything positive." It's quick, it's safe and it's simple. I was going through cash so fast that I put a self-imposed limit of $400 a day on my cash withdrawals, figuring if I needed more than that in a 24-hour period, I had a real drug problem.

This made perfect sense to me at the time. One of the craziest things about addiction is, even though you know deep down the things you're doing are wrong, in your drug-infected mind, you rationalize them to make them okay. You lie to yourself and your lies become your truth. Every drug addict I've ever known is on their way somewhere. They're finishing school, they have a job lined up, and they're getting their kids back or waiting for that inheritance check. It's all happening in the very near future and coincides with not using drugs.

The need to believe life will have a happy ending becomes the addict's reality in order to endure the horrors of their addiction in the present moment. In truth, most addicts will end up dead or in jail, with friends and family talking about what potential they had and what a waste their life had become. Most addicts I've met are fairly intelligent people with tremendous potential, but they are inflicted with a horrible disease that robs them of their natural abilities.

I think it was a combination of my insatiable curiosity, feeling of invincibility and a desire for more that made me susceptible to addiction. I wasn't a down-and-out loser with no one to love me. I wasn't a loner with no friends. I wasn't paranoid that everyone was against me and trying to hurt me. I certainly didn't know better than everyone else. But when I picked up that glass pipe, I became all of those things and within a very short span of time, that is what my reality had become.

It wasn't long before I started missing family functions and canceling visits with my daughter, who was then two years old. The visits I had with Amanda were becoming empty and I began cutting them short in order to continue getting high. As stupid as this now sounds, I had a rule of not smoking crack while I was with Amanda. It was okay to smoke before I picked her up and right after I dropped her off, but not during. This tactic led to a lot of sticking Amanda in front of the television and my passing out until it was time to take her home. I was actually admired by fellow crackheads for taking the time to see Amanda and not smoking. I should have gotten a plaque that said that and hung it on the wall.

I picked up Amanda one morning, brought her to my home and passed out in bed. I had made plans for us to hang out with my brother Adam that afternoon and when he arrived, he heard

Amanda upstairs. Adam ran up to my room and was horrified at the sight of Amanda sitting on top of me, pounding on my motionless body, yelling, "Daddy, wake up! Wake up!" He thought I was dead.

He determined I was just out cold and tried waking me, but after my being up for days, all he could get out of me was a few grunts. It was a miracle I didn't fall asleep in the car on the parkway with Amanda. He took Amanda back to Veronica's. When I woke up hours later, I realized I was all alone and freaked out. I looked all over the house trying to find Amanda. Then I saw Adam's note taped to the front door, telling me what he had done. I was so pissed off at him, I called him, screaming, "Who the fuck do you think you are, taking my daughter away like that?" I told him, "Never interfere with me again. Fuck you; I never want to see you again." Well, thank God he didn't listen to me. I love him.

This marked the beginning of a very slow turning point in my life. I began to think, after I calmed down, I might have a drug problem. To butcher a Winston Churchill quote after the British beat Rommel and drove the Germans out of Africa in World War II, "This was not the end of my addiction. It wasn't even the beginning of the end. It was, perhaps, the end of the beginning." It was the first time I realized there might be a possibility that I had a drug problem, which is the very first step in recovery: admitting you have a problem.

The importance of things like family, friends, responsibility, and personal hygiene were all still in my mind. If asked, I would have told you these were the basic elements a person needed to function in society and lead a healthy, happy life. Since I once possessed those elements, it was so easy to convince myself I still had them, but I didn't. I began to forsake everything in my life for a glass pipe and a blowjob. It's hard to describe. It's not like everything else in the world didn't matter; it still did. It was as if they were set aside for a moment, put off for just a while as

I got high, put off for another day, a tomorrow that kept getting farther and farther away.

I lived my addiction one day at a time, because tomorrow I was going to change. Those tomorrows became weeks, weeks became months, and months turned into years. Years of circling the drain, waiting for that one last hit that would wash me down into a dark sewer never to be seen again. "Yeah, I was fucking up a little bit," would be my rationale, but I could make it right and turn my life around whenever I wanted.

This is how an addict's mind works—how an addict gets through his days. It's all about the bright future when you turn your life around. I had boarded a nonstop express train to hell that I continued to ride for a few years. It was only after being arrested five times, going to jail and nearly losing everything, including the ability to see my child, that the light in my head finally turned on. They say you need to hit rock-bottom in order to begin recovery. Well, I earned a gold star at rock bottom.

Ivan Sayles

Chapter Twenty-four

Captain Ivan and First Officer Eddie

During the summer months, giant cruise ships line up at piers 88, 90 and 92 at the New York Cruise Terminal along the Hudson River on Manhattan's west side. To determine the location of a pier, subtract 40 from the pier number and that will give you the corresponding cross street within a block of the pier. Why they didn't just name them the 48th, 50th and 52nd Street piers is a mystery to me. Perhaps it was to confuse the Germans during World War II. Who the fuck knows?

These giant white behemoths dock right next to the USS Intrepid, dwarfing the World War II–era aircraft carrier that served as home for some 2,600 men for over 30 years until she was decommissioned in 1974. On a side note, it's definitely worth a visit. In addition to the tour of the carrier itself, it boasts a Concorde jet and space shuttle on its flight deck. I have no idea how they got those things on the carrier but I do remember as clear as day when they flew the space shuttle in on the back of a 747, circling Manhattan Island before landing.

Modern-day cruise ships are so big that if you stood one of them on end it would be as tall as the Empire State Building. The

New York Cruise Terminal handles 900,000 passengers a year and in the summer of 2002, I was determined to be one of them. Being a savvy internet maven, or so I like to think I am, I located a four-night/five-day bargain on Carnival Cruise Lines at a 70 percent discount. It was a last-minute deal that sailed in 10 days and after confirming the dates with my friend Eddie, it was a done deal. The ship was to set sail the following Sunday.

That Saturday, one day before our embarkation, we decided to have lunch at a beachfront restaurant looking out over the ocean, laughing and toasting about how tomorrow at that time we would be sailing in the Atlantic, cruising by that very location. We were so psyched for the trip, it was to be a first cruise for the two of us.

Sunday morning we took the Long Island Railroad to Manhattan and a taxi a few blocks west to start our vacation. The joke was on us. Since I booked it online and so close to the departure date, they didn't mail us our tickets (yes, they mailed tickets in those days). Instead, I was to pick them up at the gate. The cab dropped us off right on time on Sunday morning. There we stood on the sidewalk in our shorts and Hawaiian shirts, bags in hand, staring at three empty berths and the USS Intrepid, not a cruise ship in sight. In my haste and excitement, I had gotten the days confused and the ship had sailed the day before, on Saturday. It was probably cruising right by us the day before as Eddie and I were having lunch, whooping it up and toasting to our vacation.

We called my partner Rich, told him what happened, got back in a cab, got back on the train and headed to Rachel's to start drinking away our woes. Rich had wasted no time. The minute we walked in the door, the regulars at the bar started slapping me on the back, asking me if I could help book bargain vacations for them, too, as a captain's hat was placed on my head. When I brought my luggage to the back, there was a sign on the office door that said "Captain's Quarters."

We have an excellent reputation at Rachel's and we've won Best Seafood Restaurant on Long Island four years in a row. I'm very proud of the plates we put out, yet I believe our true talent lies not in our food but in the art of breaking balls.

OVERCOOKED

Chapter Twenty-five

It's Way Too Expensive to Be a Drug Addict

Among the hardest things for me to overcome on my journey of sobriety was to realize my powerlessness over my addiction. Accepting this and realizing I'm human and subject to all the flaws that come with that was one of the first steps of my recovery. Once clean, it then became a maintenance issue, so I use my memories to help me maintain my sobriety. I choose to look at my addiction as if looking back on high school years. There were some good times, but I was 17 years old and no matter what, I can never be 17 again; I transfer that logic to my addiction. I smoked crack and had some good times, but no matter what, I can never smoke crack again.

Some things are easy to place a value on: a gallon of gas, a pack of cigarettes or a loaf of bread. They are commodities regulated by supply and demand. Others such as time, health and life are priceless commodities where the dollar has absolutely no value. There's so much money in the world, more than anyone could possibly count in a lifetime, but what does that mean in terms of life? Absolutely nothing. The money comes, the money goes. It's insignificant. There are things money can't buy, things too valuable for currency. In other words, there are things in life too expensive even for money.

I enjoyed doing drugs. Artificial stimulants felt damn good. If it didn't feel so damn good, this country wouldn't be experiencing the addiction epidemic it vehemently refuses to deal with. But are drugs worth the price? Well, in terms of paper currency, I would have to say yes. Crack cocaine is worth the money—every penny of it. For about $150, you can buy a couple of grams of crack and get high all day. Compare that with dinner for two for around a hundred bucks at a local restaurant like, say for example, Rachel's Waterside Grill on the Nautical Mile in Freeport, NY, hint hint! Or a one-day park-hopper pass at Disney for $160, and yes, it's worth the money. Hell yeah!

But smoking crack is a high no one can afford. The price an addict pays to get high is not measured in dollars, pesos, or pounds, it's measured in the currency of life, a precious finite commodity that once spent is gone forever and can never be gotten back. There's no overtime or vacation pay to help compensate and make it better, it's just gone. For two years, I chose to spend my dollars of life getting high, thinking of no one but myself, convinced I could beat the system, certain I was in control, and worse, believing that this was the life I wanted.

It was a horrible thing, sobering up and realizing what I had become, the damage I'd done, the people I'd hurt, the time I'd thrown away and the heavy price I paid to get high. What did I have to show for it? Oh, I have plenty of memories—memories of fear, memories of arrests, memories of jail and memories of waking up in crack houses with my pockets empty. Memories of not being able to look my family and friends in the eye for fear of them seeing me for what I had become. Memories like asking my dear friend, Beverly, to watch my 4-year-old daughter because I was so busy and had "errands" to run, while the only errand I ran was buying a bag of crack and getting high. Memories of resisting any help my loved ones tried to bestow upon me.

My family and friends put together a clusterfuck of an intervention. It was done with the best of intentions but it unfortunately did not pan out. The only thing my intervention had in common with the ones you see on TV was the word "intervention." My daughter's mom, Veronica, hosted it in her apartment, but someone forgot to tell her that it was an intervention not a wine and cheese intervention party.

It was my 42nd birthday and I was invited to her apartment to have cake with Veronica and my daughter, Amanda, or so I thought. I got high that afternoon and knew I was not going to be on time. When I called to tell Veronica I'd be late and asked to speak to Amanda, I was told she was doing something in the other room or some such thing (I really don't remember), and she couldn't come to the phone at that moment. Sober, I probably would have left it at that, but one of the side effects of smoking crack is paranoia, so I began to get suspicious about what was going on. I decided to park at a building adjacent to Veronica's complex and walk over to her apartment.

When I walked in, I saw the apartment was full of family—my brother Adam, my cousins—and even my friends Vic, Rich and Eddie were there. I thought, "Wow, this is great! Is this all for me? Well, it was definitely for me, just not exactly the way I had in mind. Immediately, the whole room jumped up at me. They were in my face talking about rehab, telling me how much they loved me, and how much they cared and that I needed to stop using....

Well, maybe they jumped up and were in my face, and maybe not. I was high as a kite, so simply walking into the apartment bordered on an overwhelming task. It was out of control. Janice, my very soon-to-be ex-girlfriend and Veronica were all buzzed up, wine glasses in hand, slurring their words and telling everyone about how much they were suffering because of my addiction. Not that I hadn't put them through hell, but hey, this was supposed to be my intervention, not their pity party.

Anyway, everyone was hugging me and crying. I just couldn't take it. I thanked everyone for coming and doing this for me. As much as I would have liked, there seemed no way I was getting away with an Irish exit at this party, so I tried saying my goodbyes and went to leave. I turned back and thanked everyone again from the bottom of my heart for doing this for me, which I really did mean and still do today. I never would have accomplished recovery without the support of the people in that very room. I just wasn't ready yet.

I was in a downward spiral, for sure, but I just wasn't ready to be cured, or for an intervention. No one was going to tell me how and when I would stop using drugs. What a dick I was. I made it to the door and Vic was standing there like a defensive linemen guarding the goal line. No way was I getting past him. My anxiety was skyrocketing. All I wanted to do was leave, but they were not having any part of it.

If I had been straight, a large group of people confronting me on any subject would immediately put me on the defense, but stoned? I was starting to freak out. They were still trying to reason with an irrational and high Ivan. "A" for effort! But no one, no matter how good they are, can reason with the unreasonable.

Another thing I've seen on television interventions that differed from my wine and cheese intervention party is that during the show, the family often threatens to call the police and have the addict arrested if they don't listen to reason and go to rehab. Well, the cops were called, but not to arrest me. It was me who called the cops, telling the 911 operator that I was being held against my will.

I made a big show about calling 911 and once again tried to get past Vic. He said to me, "OK, you called the cops. They're coming, so why not just sit here a few minutes and talk until they get here?" Holy shit, Vic reasoned to the unreasonable. I calmed down and listened. To what, exactly, I don't know. I was high and can't remember. I just remember that Vic defused a very tense situation.

When the police arrived, my family had no choice but to let me go and there were no arrests. I cut out in between two buildings to get to my car, coincidently escaping the eyes of the police who had plenty of grounds to pull me over and arrest me for driving under the influence. But not before my cousin Nancy caught me for one last attempt, pleading with tearful eyes that I was going to die if I did not stop.

She was right, but I still had not hit rock bottom. I still thought I was in control. I knew better than everyone, and with that I got in my car and drove away. The only thing accomplished that night was driving an even bigger wedge between me, my family and my friends.

I had chosen to spend some of my dollars of life getting high, and all I have to show for it now are the memories of causing those closest to me, those I love the most, who cared for me and tried their best to help me, nothing but pain and heartbreak. I so wish I could have spent my dollars of life on the fond memories of blowing out birthday candles with Amanda on my 42nd birthday, but I didn't. Can I ever put a value on missing that and causing so much pain to those who loved me? I don't think so, but I can tell you that my 42nd birthday cost me a fortune.

OVERCOOKED

Chapter Twenty-six

Hold On, I'll Get You a Glass of Water

Veronica and I broke up shortly after she got pregnant; I had a quick fling with one of my waitresses, then started dating Janice. We got along great because we were both interested in the same things: drinking, sniffing coke, and getting to work on time. I finally met the perfect woman for me. I didn't acknowledge it at the time, but we were both functioning addicts going through life at half-speed.

To the outside world we led normal lives, paid our bills, went out to dinner and went on vacations. We did everything normal people did, except when everyone else went home, we ponied up a hundred bucks for coke and stayed out till 4 a.m., then showed up red-eyed and grouchy for work. You know the saying, "I wish I had a nickel for every time I did blah blah blah." Well, I wish I had a hundred bucks for every time I pissed away a hundred bucks on coke.

After a few years of dating, Janice and I bought a house and moved in together. The timing of that decision could not have been worse, as it coincided with the beginning of my transformation from coke addict to crackhead. The days of my being a functioning addict were over. We ended up closing on the house just as my addiction was peeking into full-blown junkie. My relationship with Janice was becoming unbearable. I don't know why we went through with buying the house, but we did.

Shortly after we moved into the house, her father died. I was able to get my shit together and sober up for a few days, trying to be the man I could not possibly be at that time in my life and be there for her and her family. I made it through a couple of days, helping with the funeral arrangements and the wake, and being supportive. I can remember Janice swearing to me, upon her father's death, that she would never use cocaine again, as her father would be watching over her from heaven. But as I know all too well, old habits die hard and that didn't last long.

Janice's mother was having dinner for the family at her house after the funeral. I had been doing great for a few days but just couldn't hold out. I got to her mom's late, and Janice met me at the door. I was fucked up and she knew it. She freaked out and refused to let me in the house. That was the only excuse I needed to go on a week-long bender before I showed up back at our house.

Out on a tear for that week, I ran out of money and drugs and came home at 2 a.m. in a foul mood. After two weeks' worth of artificial stimulants, I passed out for 30 hours straight. My body could no longer take the stress of going 160 hours with no sleep, sustaining myself on only a few slices of pizza and some candy bars. It was disgusting.

I had sores on my body and face from the combination of not washing and picking at myself during some paranoid delusion that something was crawling under my skin. I had previously dug a hole in my groin with a pair of tweezers that became so infected it turned into a one-inch-wide by three-inch-long abscess that had to be lanced and drained by a doctor.

I had actually thrown out all the tweezers in the house after that for fear of being on a binge and gouging myself again. I was in such bad physical shape, my face was gaunt and you could see every one of my ribs. Hygiene was almost nonexistent and I was buying black-market antibiotics to fight off the infections I was constantly getting. I started developing all kinds of ailments. I would break out in cold sweats, shivering on 80-degree days. My ankles were swollen and I was having difficulty walking; all my joints ached. But one nice hit off the glass pipe and all the pain and suffering would go away.

I remember going to the doctor one time with a swollen ankle. I had been up for days as usual, looking emaciated, with scabs all over my face and body from picking at myself. I left the office to get my bloodwork done and when I went back for the follow-up appointment, I noticed the doctor was acting a little strange. He was standoffish and I got the feeling he didn't want to talk to me. I was told my white blood cell count was dangerously low, which is a sign of a diminished immune system, and he suggested I have an HIV test immediately. He couldn't wait to get me out of his office.

I took the test and by the grace of God, it came up negative. Since I'd stick my dick in just about anything when I was high, I honestly don't know how the Grim Reaper missed me. For years, I had been playing Russian roulette, fucking more crack whores than I will ever be able to remember. That was my modus operandi. I'd pick up some shit, pick up a girl, get a room, get high and fuck 'til the drugs ran out—or I got bored.

After three or four days of partying, the only thing that kept me going was another hit. But eventually even the drugs couldn't keep me awake and I would crash. No matter what I was doing or where I was. Nothing could control the inevitable passing out, when the body finally says enough is enough. As my body would begin shutting down, I would start hallucinating and mumbling gibberish. Kind of like when you're just nodding off to sleep and someone asks you a question and you respond, "The blue marbles are eating helicopters."

You know the feeling: it happens to most people after only one sleepless night. You're in front of the computer, or watching late-night TV, or worse, driving your car. Your eyes start getting droopy and your head starts to wobble and dip, the muscles in your neck don't seem strong enough to keep your head upright anymore. Your skull feels heavier and heavier, then finally your neck gives out, your head plummets to the ground, then, SNAP! Your neck comes back to life at the last second and pops your head back up.

This happens to everyone. But it doesn't usually happen when you're in the middle of a sentence. I can remember being asked questions and halfway through my answers, I would forget what I was talking about or even what the questions were. Just like that, I would start rambling delusional speech.

After you've deprived yourself of sleep for a few days, strange things start happening, including uncontrollable muscle contractions; physically, you just can't take it anymore. Your body says to the brain, "Enough! I'm tired and I want to go to bed." But the brain, high on the stimulants from cocaine, doesn't agree. It sends a bolt of electricity down your spine like a cattle prod shocking your muscles and causing them to snap and convulse. Your brain is telling your body, fuck you—if I'm not sleeping, ain't nobody sleeping.

After the drugs ran out, the withdrawal would inevitably lead to a crack hangover, which consisted of bad temperament, anger, depression and feelings of self-loathing, which made me one hell of a mess stumbling through the door at 2 a.m. By this time in our relationship, Janice was never really glad to see me anyway, never mind in crack hangover mode.

That particular evening after we had been cohabitating in the same house for about eight months, when I got home instead of using the front door like a normal person, I went in through the garage. Why? Because I was a dick, that's why. Our two-car garage had electric garage door openers, and the motor on the left-hand side was conveniently located directly beneath the bed in the master bedroom above, and Sears had designed their garage door opener motors for longevity, not silence.

I walked in through the garage into the house wearing my best shit-eating smirk and Janice was right where I wanted her, at the top of the stairs, screaming. Well, we got right into it, yelling at each other face to face. I could smell the booze on her breath. The fight evolved from one subject to another, including her going on a rant about my addiction, each of us blaming the other for everything and neither of us listening to what the other had to say.

At this point, it was still a typical fight between a man and a woman. The more we got into it, however, the more unstable I became, to the point where I was just a ranting, irrational lunatic. We began the second half of the hour still screaming, insulting and belittling one another in every room in the house. By now we were upstairs arguing in the hallway and Janice was saying how she couldn't take it anymore and she just wanted out of all this. I was on a roll, and Janice was folding. Naturally, I turned it up to full throttle. Attack! Attack! Attack! I was relentless.

Our fight landed us in the upstairs bathroom and Janice was going berserk. She started opening cabinets and popping pills, screaming that she wanted to end her life. By this time, any semblance of a normal human being had left my drug-starved body and I was incapable of rational thought. Janice was now popping open every pill bottle in the cabinet, knocking them back like shots of whiskey, choking as she swallowed them dry. I did what now seems like the cruelest, most heartless thing anyone could ever do at a time like this. I went downstairs, poured a glass of water, brought it up to her and went to bed.

I don't know what woke me up. Maybe my guilt was stronger than my need for sleep, but somehow, a short time later I awoke and went into Janice's room to check on her. She was lying face down on the bed, drooling. I tried shaking her and talking to her, but she was lethargic and unresponsive. All I could get out of her were a few grunts. I figured it was a good idea to get her to a hospital.

Every time I tried lifting her, she slid down through my hands like liquid. I was starting to get nervous about her condition and how I would be able to even get her down the full flight of stairs then into the car once I got her down the stairs. I temporarily gave up on her and went to position the car so when I got her out of the house I could easily get her into it. I found the keys to her Jeep, and figuring I could never get her into the front seat, I backed it into the driveway and popped open the rear hatch and went back upstairs.

This time, when I touched her, she sprang back to life, popped right up like a human jack-in-the-box, kicking and screaming: "Don't you fucking touch me!" and "Get the fuck away from me." I couldn't get near her. Then she seemed to pass out again but the second I touched her, it would happen all over again. I didn't know what to do. I called one of her friends, Kerry, in the hope that she could get Janice to go to the hospital.

By the time Kerry showed up, I had passed out again, this time downstairs on the couch. Kerry woke me and we went upstairs together to try and deal with Janice, but we got the same results I did when I was by myself. Every time we touched her body, she sprang to life, kicking and screaming. There seemed to be nothing else we could do, so I called 911 and went back to bed.

The next thing I knew two cops were standing next to my bed, screaming at me to wake up. They immediately started badgering me with questions. It took me a few moments to get it together and realize what was happening. As I was becoming coherent again, I tried to get up, but they told me to sit back down. I wanted to leave the room, but they were having no part of that. They insisted I stay seated on the bed while they asked me questions—but they started feeling more like accusations than questions.

I didn't understand. I didn't do anything wrong. They wanted to know what I was planning to do. Where was I planning on going? What had I given Janice? Why was the car backed up in the driveway with the tailgate popped open? I had the corner pieces but didn't quite get the whole puzzle yet.

Suddenly it all made sense. If there was a shovel in the back of her car, I would have been arrested on the spot. Who knows what Kerry, not a big fan of mine, by the way, and the cops were talking about before they woke me up. I'm sure my tumultuous relationship with Janice and drug addiction were hot topics. I explained to the police what had happened and how I planned on taking her to the hospital, and the reason I had backed up the car. I was the one who called 911, for Christ's sake!

By this time, Janice was coming around and pretty much confirmed that this was not attempted murder, so the cops started lightening up on me a bit. Janice refused to go to the hospital, but the police said it was mandatory in a case like this. So she went, got her stomach pumped, had blood work done and received a nice little psych evaluation. Thank God we had nothing stronger than Ambien, aspirin, antibiotics and a couple of Xanax in the medicine cabinet. She never spent another night in our house.

OVERCOOKED

Chapter Twenty-seven

Arrest Number Four

This story you are about to read is true, only the names have been changed to protect the innocent or, in this case, the not-so-innocent.

On August 15, 2008, I'd like to tell you I was sitting at home quietly minding my own business, but that would be a lie. Janice had moved out and I was now free to do whatever in the house. My drug habit was peaking and I was in the process of redecorating the house with crack pipes and whores. Janice came over that afternoon to check her mail and as she pulled into the driveway I ran out of the house. There was no way I was letting her leave without a fight. Before she even got out of the car, I was all over her. Who knows what I was raging about? I was the one who fucked her over. Why was I mad at her?

It didn't take long for the argument to get out of hand, and I ended up smashing the side-view mirror off her car. She called the police, who at this point were very familiar with my address. Janice insisted they arrest me, but instead they decided to mitigate—a more reasonable solution. We came to an agreement on the value of the mirror and I paid Janice $160 for it. The police filled out a report that we both signed, indicating I had made financial restitution and that no arrest was necessary.

I don't know how Janice did what she did next. She got a lawyer and went to the police station the next day and spoke to Detective Macanudo. The detective took a new deposition stating the events of August 15, which was one sided and different from the report taken at the scene. The new report caused an arrest warrant to be issued. At some point another brave detective, Robert Henry, took over the case.

I have done more than my share of wrong and have paid for my crimes according to the laws of New York State and Nassau County. I would like to make it known that I have the utmost respect and appreciation for the honest, brave, hard-working men and women of our nation's police departments. Thank you for your service and sacrifices. These men and women swore an oath to protect and serve with honesty and integrity. I, along with most citizens, did not. What I don't respect and consider the lowest form of criminal are the scumbags who violate that oath, the crooked cops. I am of the opinion that all police officers, whether on or off duty, should be held to a level of accountability equal to the power bestowed upon them. With great power comes great responsibility. It was your choice to do what you do and we citizens entrust you with our safety and well-being.

Three months later, on November 8, 2008, the police came to my house to arrest me for breaking Janice's mirror. I was in the house getting high as usual, with a female companion, smoking a particular batch of crack that made us very paranoid. Since there is no industry standard for crack, it often differs, giving slightly different highs with each batch. Maybe it's what they cut it with, or the strain of the coca plant from which it's produced? I'll never know, nor do I care much anymore. But some batches of crack got me extremely paranoid and some did not. That one we were smoking was a particularly paranoid batch.

The dog kept barking. I was hearing car doors opening and shutting all afternoon and kept seeing strangers walking in front of my house. In the end it wasn't really paranoia: the police were staking out the house in preparation of arresting me, but I didn't know that yet. I just thought I was being delusional from smoking so much crack. I would go downstairs every half-hour or so to make sure all the doors' locks were bolted. I even went as far as getting my screw gun and drilled screws in my front door to seal it shut. Now that I finally felt secure in my home, I settled in to get high. I stripped down to my boxer shorts and lay down in bed with my female companion for some smoking.

Shortly thereafter, some of the cops started pounding on the door and telling me to open up. Believing they had no right to enter my home, I refused. But they had a back-up plan: they had Janice. Janice and I owned the house together, so when I refused to let them enter, she handed them a key and said go right in. I can only imagine their frustration when they couldn't open the door due to my screws.

At that point there was lots of shouting back and forth and then Janice gave them permission to break the window and enter the house. I was screaming that I did not give permission for them to enter. Janice and the cops won. As they broke the window and officer Tymes began climbing in, I heard an officer say something about resisting arrest, so I put my hands straight up in the air and chanted, "I am not resisting arrest…you do not have permission to enter my house," over and over.

Officer Tymes got in the house as the other officers were trying to break down the front door, while I was backing away from the window, continuing my chant. Realizing at this point I had lost, and not wanting to get the shit beaten out of me, I told officer Tymes that I had screwed the door shut and asked him if he wanted me to remove the screws. He said yes. He did not put me in handcuffs or make any move toward me. He let me get my screw gun off the counter and unblock the door. The moment the door was open, the cops flew in, tackled and handcuffed me. They stood me up against the wall as our hero, brave Detective Henry, walked in.

He was a tall man, about 6' 3", and dressed in slacks and a Columbo-style overcoat. He stood next to me, looking up and down at my handcuffed, emaciated 145-pound body, standing nose against the wall. I could see his arm recoiling. "Asshole!" he yelled as his fist came crashing down on my face, knocking me to the ground into the broken glass from the front window. By this time there were cops everywhere.

They dragged me outside in my boxer shorts and put me in the back of a patrol car. A uniformed officer came out and handed me a shirt, shoes and pants he had gotten from my bedroom, so I could get dressed. I inspected the clothes, including the pockets of the pants they had given me. They were empty. They uncuffed me, allowed me to dress, re-cuffed me and put me back in the car. I happened to live about four blocks from the 7th precinct, so it was a short ride to the station for processing. When we got there I was put into a holding cell until officers John Tymes and Carm Fell took me out and told me they were going to strip-search me. I thought I was going to be brought into a room that was set up for this type of thing, but instead they walked me to the bathroom of the precinct. As I entered, they closed the bathroom door and I began mentally getting ready for the beating I was sure I was going to get. I was told to take off my clothes. I handed my pants to officer Fell as officer Tymes told me to turn around and face him. As I did so, he told me to squat and stand up. I obeyed. I was naked, but no one had thrown a punch at me. So far, so good! They told me to turn back around and as I did, officer Feil was pulling a baggie of white powder out of the pocket of my jeans, asking me, "What is this Here?" These two clowns had tried to plant a bag of shit on me. Let's think about this for a minute. The cops arrested me in my boxers and brought me clothes from my house. Once this lightbulb went on, I started to get a little cocky. I reminded them I was arrested in my underwear and that I searched the pockets when a cop brought me my pants, as I'm sure the officer who brought me my clothes did before he gave them to me. Then they got all defensive and asked if I was accusing them of planting drugs in my pants pocket.

Suddenly I came back to my senses, realizing I was locked in a bathroom of the 7th precinct, naked, with two crooked cops who obviously had it in for me, so I backed down real quick. Our argument continued as I got dressed. When they opened the door, I regained some confidence and we started arguing again in the hallway. They were waving the baggie in my face, telling me, "We'll see what happens when we get this back from the lab." Then they brought me upstairs and chained me to a bench while they did their paperwork.

I couldn't see them from where I was, but I could hear them talking. I heard them say that the detective wanted me charged with resisting arrest. I heard one cop ask the other how he should write it up. The answer I heard was, "Look in the computer for the one we did last week and copy that one. Just change the names and dates."

I requested a trip to the hospital to get my leg checked out, as it was still bleeding from when I had gotten punched and fell into the broken glass. They obliged, then off to central booking. When I was arraigned in the morning, there was no mention of any sort of possession charges. Looking back at the situation, it all makes sense. I found out later, when the uniformed officer asked the woman in the house for pants to bring me, she searched the pockets, handed the officer my pants, and he searched them, as well. You would think that would be standard operating procedure for the cops to search clothes before they give them to a prisoner, lest there is a weapon or something in one of my pockets. So finding shit on me in the precinct would have been utterly ridiculous. Those were the positives that morning. I would just have to wait and see how my lawyer handled the criminal mischief and resisting arrest charges.

As the days went by, this planting of shit on me by Thymes and Fell just didn't sit right with me. My best guess was that there was about 5 grams of white powder in that bag. Being caught with that amount of cocaine would have gotten me 3-5 years in jail. After recounting my story of arrest to my crack buddies, one of my fellow smokers told me the same cops had planted stuff on him six months earlier and he had gotten arrested. A girl told me these two bozos pulled her over and Tymeck tried to pick her up. True stories or not, it got my blood boiling. Then I started thinking, who did these men think they were? I had never done anything to harm them or their families. I had never met them before November 8, 2008. Yet they were willing to plant shit on me that would have sent me to jail for several years. They were willing to rob me of 3-5 years of my life because they could. No one should have such power.

I was enraged. I called the Internal Affairs Unit of the Nassau County Police Department to make a complaint. I met with an investigator and told him the story. He asked me to identify the officers from pictures, of which one I was positive, but the other picture looked like it was from his police academy graduation. I asked for a better picture, but he had none to offer. He just told me to do my best. He asked why I came forward with this. I explained to him that even though no charges were filed, the fact that this was done enraged me. It ended up working out in my favor this time, but if circumstances were different, it could have gone badly for me. He asked for some background on me and I was truthful about my addiction. He wrote down everything I said. He seemed sincere in his concerns and said he would interview all the officers involved and get back to me. In March of 2009, I got a letter from the district attorney's office that said, "The evidence does not warrant a criminal prosecution of any member of the Nassau County Police Department."

This was not the last I would see of Tymes and Fell. They would arrest me again around the corner from my house and play their dirty little games with the woman whose car I was in.

Chapter Twenty-eight

The Little Blue Pill That Saved Rachel's

I bought Rachel's in December of 1996 and with the fiasco of the first few days behind me, it was time to change the image of the Texas Ranger to that of a new American-style seafood restaurant. Subsequently, I spent the remainder of my life savings on renovations doing just that. By the time the summer of '97 rolled around, business was pretty good, to which I attributed my prowess as a restaurateur. In reality, I found out that fall, it had really been nothing more than a little buzz created over a new Nautical Mile restaurant and increasingly better weather, as spring turned to summer.

All in all, my first summer in business was pretty good despite the streets flooding on several weekends. What I wasn't prepared for was the tremendous drop in business come Labor Day. It was like someone pulled the rug right out from under me. To this day, I don't understand why so many people stop coming down to the waterfront after Labor Day. September and October are hands down the best time of the year to dine on the water on Long Island. The hot, sticky air of August is replaced by dry, cooler air in the 70s with clear, crisp, blue skies. I've tried to figure this out for years. People say the kids are back in school and families are settling back into their routine. I say bullshit! None of that stopped them from coming in the spring. Why should it stop them now?

I kept a full staff on through September, figuring this business would pick right back up after the Jewish holidays, but it didn't. It just began a slow decline from September through October. I did my best to hang on and sucked up my losses. Then winter came and it got even worse. In those days after New Year's, half of the restaurants on the block would shut down for the winter and reopen a couple of months later in the spring. I chose to stay open that first winter, and to this day we're still open all year.

It was a conscious business decision to preserve the consistency of our product and service. By staying open year 'round, I retained my staff and didn't have to train a brand new crew every season. There is one other reason: I've always had a great sense of loyalty and responsibility to my employees, especially those who stayed with me through the years of my addiction. To some, Rachel's is a second job, to others it's a stepping stone to another career, but to many it's their livelihood. They have husbands or wives, children and mortgages. To shut down for two months and go to Florida while my staff sits at home and struggles to get by with an unemployment check is just not an option for me. It never was.

I didn't need my accountant to sum up the financials of my first 15 months in business and tell me it was a disaster. For the first five months, I operated at a loss while investing my life savings into improvements. That was followed by a profitable summer, which was nice, but there was not enough profit to carry me through the next winter of losses. Each week, I kept pouring more money back into Rachel's.

It was the end of March 1998, and my life savings was practically gone. I was $100,000 in debt and getting desperate. I tried everything I could think of. These were the days before Groupon and LivingSocial were forced into extinction, such terms as Two'fers, early birds and buy one–get one free were commonplace at restaurants desperate for business. I'm not saying that these promotions don't have their place, but if a restaurant has an 'all you can eat pasta night' on a Saturday, that could be a sign of desperation. I asked Chris, my chef, if he had ever won any awards. He told me he had won an award for perfect attendance back in high school. Perfect! We now had an award-winning chef and I made sure all our advertising made that abundantly clear.

I used to stare out the window watching cars drive by my store on weekend nights, only to drive past in the other direction a few minutes later. I'm not saying hundreds of cars did this, but enough did for me to notice a pattern. I soon realized they were driving to the end of the block to the Schooner, a 200-seat well-established restaurant that closed for the winter. Desperate for business, I had to come up with a way to get those drive-bys into my parking lot.

To quote a Franciscan friar named Ockham, "The simplest solution is most likely the right one." So on weekends, I would drive down the block to the Schooner and right under the sign that they had hung saying, "Closed for the Season – Will Reopen in April," I put up my own sign saying, "Try Rachel's Waterside Grill," then take it down on my way home. We got quite a few customers from that marketing campaign. When one customer came in and mentioned they saw the sign on the Schooner and it was their first time trying us, I simply replied, "That's very nice, we're all friends down here."

Ultimately it was a drug, a little blue pill that saved Rachel's from financial ruin. Now, don't go thinking I have another vice I haven't told you about. But it was definitely a drug that caused Rachel's to get noticed and bring in new customers. It was Viagra.

You see, Pfizer had just released Viagra, and it was a tremendous success. It was a miracle drug for guys who couldn't get it up. It was all over television and newspapers, and one morning

OVERCOOKED

while driving to work, I was listening to a radio news program and they were interviewing the woman in charge of the advertising campaign for Viagra. Pfizer had just announced a huge, hundred-some-odd million-dollar advertising budget for the pill.

The interviewer asked the Pfizer representative, why such a huge budget? Everyone knew about Viagra: the news media had done plenty of free advertising for the little blue pill. Was it really necessary to spend that much? The advertising executive's reply was something I'll never forget. She said, "Right now we're at the top of the hill, but our competitors will be climbing up to try to knock us off, and we want to stay on top. Other versions of erectile dysfunction drugs will soon be on the market and we want to make sure we retain our share." She went on to say that "Everyone in the world knows McDonald's sells hamburgers, yet they spend billions in advertising every year."

Bingo! I needed to get the word out and spend some money on advertising. I started reading everything I could get my hands on about advertising. It turned out Hofstra University was having a seminar on advertising, sponsored by some small business organization. I thought the seminar was great and the price certainly fit my budget: it was free.

At the seminar, they went over budgeting and average amounts different industries spend on advertising, techniques for getting your message out and the importance of repetition. Two of the guest speakers particularly impressed me. They were two women who were partners in a Long Island real estate agency. They said the average advertising budget for the real estate industry was between 2 and 5 percent of sales.

When they decided they wanted to grow from a $10 million a year company into a $20 million company, they doubled their advertising budget to that of a $20 million dollar company and consequently doubled their sales. I adopted their technique and that spring went on a huge advertising blitz, including using my last bit of money to shoot and run a television commercial for Rachel's.

Cablevision still had a monopoly on TV on Long Island, and was in a huge expansion mode, adding channels to its lineup like crazy. Channels like Lifetime, E, and the Food Network were all up-and-coming. Cablevision was adding so many channels so fast that they were not selling out all their advertising spots. As my dumb luck would have it, I discovered something called auto-fill.

Auto-fill is pretty much exactly what it sounds like. Television shows for the most part are pre-recorded with commercial breaks fit into the programming. Even live shows break for commercials at predetermined time slots. If a network does not sell all its commercial spots during a particular show, they need to fill the slots, otherwise it would be just dead air. They fill in those blank spots randomly with the commercials they already have in inventory. That's why sometimes when you're watching TV late at night, you'll see the same ad over and over every commercial break. The network probably had empty slots and needed to fill them.

I was able to buy one or two commercial spots a week on a network that wasn't selling out and sometimes get up to 20 spots a week for the price of just two. I was even able to buy a one-minute spot on the Sports Channel for a Mets-Yankee game (pre-YES Network), for $125.00. I started doing print ads in the local papers. I was getting the word out and people started coming. Once I had them in the door, we never had problems getting them to come back!

My advertising campaign was a success. So much so, that some customers would tell me they came to try us out because they heard our ad on the radio. I'd tell them that was great, thank them for coming and seat them at their table with a smile. I had never advertised on the radio at that point, but who gives a shit?

I had put a new customer in a seat that was empty. We'd give them delicious food and great service and they'd come back. I had done the math a few years prior and figured out it costs me around $16 per chair, per day to stay in business. Asses in seats, that's the name of the game in the restaurant business.

Unbeknownst to me at the time, I would need this advertising blitz once again to help to save Rachel's a second time, when I came back from my addiction. But for now, I was off to the races; business was getting better and better. My advertising got them in the door and the food and staff made sure they came back. I had done it, I had survived. I was going into my second summer and business was good. I was young and ambitious, but most importantly, I was slowly realizing I didn't know it all, although foolishly, I still thought I knew more than most. Time to buy a second restaurant!

Chapter Twenty-nine

Sometimes You Have to Drop Back and Punt: Losing My Family's Home

The son of Russian immigrants, my father grew up in Brooklyn, NY, one of four brothers. The oldest, Uncle George, I only knew from the picture of him in his Marine dress blues that was proudly hung on the wall at the top of our stairwell. Uncle Archie and Uncle George served our country bravely in World War II. Archie, now 93, was a gunner, hanging out the side of a PBY "Flying Boat" in the Navy, and George was killed in Iwo Jima.

My uncle Howard, who could not join the Army because of an ulcer, built Liberty ships to help the cause and my father, the youngest of the four, joined the Army during the Korean War. My father and his brothers were first-generation born in the United States, middle-class Americans, proud and family oriented. After his time in the service, my father married and went on to become a New York City elementary school teacher for some 35 years.

My mother, also from Brooklyn, was one of two sisters, and passed away when I was in the fifth grade. Unfortunately, I have very few memories of her other than her soft voice, gentle mannerisms and her whacking me with a wooden kitchen spoon when "enough was enough." Unable to have children of their own, my parents adopted me when I was 3 months old.

I'm not sure where they lived before I came on the scene, but they moved into a high-rise apartment building on Beach-some-thing-or-other Street in Far Rockaway, across from the boardwalk along the Atlantic Ocean. For the first four years of my life, I lived in a second-floor apartment with a balcony overlooking the ocean slightly southwest of Kennedy Airport and in line with runway 4L-22R, placing our building at the beginning or end of most flights coming in and out of NYC.

I have spotty memories of my childhood. There are huge gaps in time; some memories are as crystal clear as if they happened yesterday and some are just a spark of a recollection that I can't fully put together. I still have a vague memory of the day we picked up my sister Eve. I can remember the excitement of the day and waiting in a car that was parked along a tall black wrought-iron fence. Eve and I didn't come from the same set of parents or birth mother, but still we were brother and sister, son and daughter, family.

Shortly after Eve arrived, my father, who had been considering a new career as an air traffic controller, and my mother, who was juggling two young kids in a tiny apartment, wisely decided to move out "East" to Bellmore, a suburb on Long Island. They bought a house on a quiet cul-de- sac in a development of similar-looking brick houses. They were not Levitt homes, like many in the surrounding areas; they were split-level brick houses whose only real source of individuality was which side of the house the driveway was on, whether or not the owner had purchased the fireplace upgrade or if there were two or three shrubs along the walkway from the driveway to the front door.

It was a nice, middle-class neighborhood and our house was within walking distance to the elementary school, junior high school, supermarket and post office. The Long Island Rail Road was not too far off. It was 1969, the tracks had not yet been elevated or electrified, and on quiet nights you could hear the diesels roaring over the tracks in the distance. There were still working farms in the neighborhood and some of the secondary roads in our area, which had been built in the '50s, had not yet been paved, and didn't get paved until they put in sewers in the mid-'70s.

I grew up in an atmosphere where my parents' business was their business and none of our business. Whenever I would inquire as to the cost of something or ask if it was expensive, I always got the same answer: "It costs a dollar three-eighty." In other words, it's none of your fucking business. I also cannot ever remember seeing my parents argue or fight. Not that they didn't fight; it just wasn't done in front of the kids. It wasn't until 1999 when my dad and stepmom had a mortgage-burning celebration that I found out that the principal and interest payment on the house was $420 a month. Peanuts today, but my father had to work three jobs in order to afford it and support a family with five kids.

I have to say, growing up, I wanted for nothing. I was clothed, fed and had a roof over my head. I never got the best of anything, but I was always provided for. My bike was a Huffy, not a Schwinn. My jeans were the store brand, not Levi's. I did forget to mention the exception to the "none of our business how much it cost" rule. I was made keenly aware as to how much it cost to heat or air condition the "entire neighborhood" when I shut the screen door but forgot to close the main door to the house.

"You know how much it cost?" My father would ask. "I'll tell you. A fortune!" The second thing my dad taught me about money was "it didn't grow on trees," although I'm sure I would have figured that one out myself, given time, but he felt the need to carve that into my brain as soon I learned to speak.

A dinner out for us was Nathan's or Chinese. A special dinner out was Beefsteak Charlie's or Cookie's Steak House, probably because the latter two had all-you-can-eat salad bars and unlimited soda, beer, wine or sangria.

One thing I specifically remember growing up with was a unique set of drinking glasses embossed with a capital "S" for our last name, Sayles. The glasses had a design of what looked like wheat encircling the "S." I assumed they had been passed down from my grandparents; maybe we were descendants from royalty or something. I was very proud of those glasses and I always made sure I served my friends their drinks in our "S" glasses. It wasn't until we were on vacation one year that I realized the "S" glasses in our home were stolen from the Sheraton Hotel chain, and all my dreams of royalty were instantly shattered.

It's only now that I can look back and appreciate how hard my father worked to raise his family. I can't even imagine the pride he must have felt, being the first member of his family to ever own his own home in the suburbs. In addition to teaching, he worked part-time in Roosevelt Field Mall at Alexander's, a department store that long ago went bankrupt along with other Long Island icons such as Two Guys and Pergament. He also worked on weekends as a waiter for a catering company where I started working as a busboy when I was 14. We were a one-car family until Dad got a brand new 1974 Ford Pinto, upgraded with a CB radio. Mom had recently gotten her driver's license and got the hand-me-down Buick Skylark. She passed away the following summer from ovarian cancer.

Several years later, my father married a woman with three kids: Russ, who was my age; Gayle, who was two years younger; and Adam, who, as luck would have it, was Eve's age and in the same grade. My father renovated the garage, turning it into living space. He remodeled the den into a bedroom, so the house could accommodate a family of seven. We spent our grade school years in our home, my new siblings and I growing up, and growing just as close as any blood relations. Your family is who you make it, not whose genes you share.

As we grew older, we moved out of the house one by one. Everyone but me got married and had kids. I eventually moved back home, turning the downstairs bedrooms into an apartment for myself. With the house mostly empty and my parents getting on in years, they decided to buy a condo and sell me the house. We all hoped one day I would settle down, get married, and raise my family in our house. Unfortunately, that was not meant to be.

I met my daughter's mother, Veronica, one night in a local Bellmore bar. We started talking, laughing, playing joker poker and sniffing coke 'til the wee hours. We really hit it off. I remember thinking this must be kismet when in conversation, we discovered that before we met we had both bought identical 2003 Nissan Pathfinders. The only difference was that hers was red and mine, tan. As the night got later, we exchanged numbers, and agreed to see each other again.

Veronica and I looked great on paper. We were both young and at good points in our careers. I was in my mid 30s and she was about 32. I was a successful businessman with two restaurants and the catering contract on a gambling boat. She was an assistant vice president for JP Morgan Chase. She was living in a one-bedroom apartment in Islip when we started dating and within five months, she had moved in with me. This is where the fairytale ends, folks. The next year was a nightmare. Veronica and I kept breaking up and getting back together. I don't know what kept making us go back to each other. Even to this day we can't share so much as an opinion.

Through all that, somehow Veronica and I managed to have a wonderful baby girl together. Amanda has no idea what I have gone through or how close she came to not having a father at all. That little girl had no idea of the strength and determination she was able to give to me and in effect save my life.

While Veronica was pregnant, she moved back in with her father, then back with me, out to my house in Southampton and eventually toward the end of her pregnancy, I bought an apartment in Suffolk County for her and Amanda to live in. Somewhere along the line, while she was pregnant, I started dating Janice.

Janice and I dated for about four years, although I don't know if I would consider the fourth year dating so much as being reluctant living companions stuck in a bad situation. Like birds of a feather, we started flocking together with groups of friends who also did coke and became very comfortable hanging out with other cokeheads, and cokeheads with kids.

It's hard sometimes to think about what I did, let alone write about it. We could be at a family barbeque, pull a hot dog off the grill, drink a beer and then go into the house and do a quick bump of coke in the bathroom.

Sooner or later, someone would scream at the kids and tell them to get outside and play in the yard and then we would just cut up some lines on the coffee table. This was terrible. It wasn't just us sniffing coke: this was different, because there were children involved. What if something happened to the kids while we were all high in the house? Or worse, what if one of the kids accidentally got ahold of some of our coke? Yet, here I was thinking I had finally found the perfect woman and circle of friends... responsible drug addicts.

After Janice and I bought the house together and moved in with each other I rented the upstairs of my parents' house to a family with two kids, and the apartment downstairs to my brother-in-law. I had paid off the mortgage and secured a $300,000 equity line on the house. This is a great position to be in for a normal person, but bad for a drug addict, whose need for getting high far outweighs his need for fiscal responsibility.

Additionally, property taxes, which were about $12,000 a year and were normally included in a mortgage payment, are not included in equity loans. It's the responsibility of the homeowner to pay the property taxes, which proved disastrous for me. Who wants to pay property taxes when they're busy smoking crack cocaine?

By the time we moved into our new home, things between Janice and me had gone sour. We never even shared a bedroom or had sex there, which is usually the first thing a couple does when walking into a new home. I don't even remember giving her so much as a kiss in that house.

I can't say that she and I didn't try to work things out. We did. I just hadn't hit rock bottom yet and wasn't ready to change. Janice and I were still on speaking terms for my first two attempts at recovery. She had sworn off coke completely after her father passed, and developed what I call the holier-than-thou attitude. It's the attitude that some former drug addicts, alcoholics or ex-cigarette smokers develop. Although they used drugs, drank or smoked every day for 20-some-odd years, now they're clean. All of a sudden they feel anyone who does what they no longer do is beneath them, a lowlife, a weak person with no self-control, not worthy of being given the time of day. I can't stand people like that.

How can you be critical of someone else when you yourself have walked down the same path for so long? When I relapsed, she looked down her nose at me. She wanted nothing to do with me and felt she was so much better than I was. Swearing off cocaine after her father died was a joke; it didn't last two months. One day during my recovery—the recovery she was so insistent about and supportive of—I came home and she was sniffing coke with a friend of hers in our house. There was a rolled up dollar bill and some coke right on the kitchen counter, so what did I do? I joined the party. Needless to say, that incident catapulted me right back into another crack binge. Not her fault, but I'm just saying...

Coinciding with my crack binge, the family that had been renting the upstairs portion of my parents' home bought a house of their own and moved out. What could be better? I was so fucked up at that point, I instantly turned my family home into a crack den. I furnished it with the bare essentials like a TV, bed and couch. I would drive to Hempstead with a friend, pick up a couple of girls, bring them back to the house, smoke crack and fuck for days. We would trade partners or take turns fucking the same girl. It didn't matter.

I used to laugh about getting my dick sucked and taking a hit at the same time, saying it was my favorite sport, which it was. When we were done with the girls, we'd put them in a cab and send them on their way. We'd crash, wake up and start all over again. One particular night, a crack buddy of mine, Tony, asked me for a girl's number. I was a little reluctant at first, seeing as how she was one of my main girls, but he was adamant. "Come on, Ivan, if you're not using it tonight, why can't I?" As I look back on those days I can best describe it as disgustingly mutually beneficial.

We all used each other and took advantage of each other's weaknesses. This went on in the house my parents bought, the very house that held their hopes and dreams of their children having a better life than they did. The home I was raised in was now desecrated by me with drugs and whores.

Slowly but surely, my paycheck wasn't enough to support my habit and the habits of others. Since no one else had any money and I wanted to party, I started dipping into the home equity and stopped paying my property taxes, or other bills. The cable, electricity and water would periodically get shut off in my house. I would go to the bank and get the money to get them turned right back on. I was the jackass who didn't pay the bill, but no one saw it that way; I was the hero who got the lights back on, further elevating my status to my drug addict friends.

It wasn't until the winter of 2011, when I was sober, broke and in debt that I started to compile the damage of what I had done. With interest, I owed almost $80,000.00 in back taxes and had maxed out my $300,000.00 credit line. Nassau County sold my tax lien to a private company, L&L Holdings, which was now assessing interest to my debt to the tune of 10 percent every six months.

I was at the beginning of the end of my recovery, meaning my relapses had not fully disappeared, but I was definitely spending more time not using than using. I fixed up the house for rental, modified the loan and got new tenants. I had enough cash flow to stay afloat, but I needed to come up with a good plan to start paying down the debt on the house. I wasn't making a profit, but it was doable for the time being, and I would be able to keep the house.

It wasn't until I finally got my shit together and was back to work, that I realized Rachel's was in worse financial shape than I was. To prevent the bank from foreclosing on Rachel's, I had to use the rent money I collected on my house to pay Rachel's expenses. Once again, I defaulted on the loan and sent the house into foreclosure. It was a tough decision. I knew if I used the money from my home to pay Rachel's bills, there would be no way to save my house. But if I didn't, I would lose the restaurant and the house would fall shortly thereafter, anyway.

Through outstanding work by my lawyer, Donna, who has also been a friend and source of support through my sobriety, I was able to modify both Rachel's mortgage and the equity line again to prevent foreclosure from the banks. Unfortunately, we were unable to reach a deal to pay off the debit with L&L Holdings, and they commenced foreclosure proceedings. Donna did manage to stave off foreclosure for a year while I got back on my feet, but in the end I just didn't have enough time to come up with the money to save the house.

I put my family's home up for sale and was lucky enough to find a buyer. Donna was able to stall the foreclosure for a few more months while we waited for their mortgage to get approved. On April 26, 2012, I sold my parents' home. It was a home that I once had over $300,000 equity in; the home that was the pride of my family. I walked away from the closing table still owing $8,300.00 in commission to the real estate broker. The realtor, Micky, also a friend, agreed to take the balance of her commission in payments from me. So for the next five months I made payments on a home I no longer owned.

I have to say that once again, my really good bad luck prevailed. I had the misfortune of losing the house I grew up in, the shame of being the success story of my family only to become a junkie and then lose my parents' dream home. But the house, in its final months, was able to save the restaurant and help put me back on the road to success. The loss of my family's house was not the result of the recession, falling home prices, or unemployment. The loss was my own fault, a direct result of my drug addiction. I feel immense regret and disappointment over this and many of the other things I've done but unfortunately, once things are done they are done.

My apologies, Sir Isaac Newton, but I believe your theory was wrong. For every action there is not always an equal and opposite reaction. For three years I wasted my life on drugs and it would take more than double that to get my life back, yet some things like my family's home will just be lost forever.

Ivan Sayles

Chapter Thirty

The Stewards

Working at the Jones Beach Boardwalk Restaurant was one of the most inspirational periods of my life. I formed friendships that have lasted over 35 years and most of my practical restaurant education came from my days at the beach. I learned all the tricks they cannot possibly teach you in school—especially the scams by employees, as well as tricks purveyors used to rip customers off. I didn't know it at the time, but learning all those scams would later provide me the skills to know what to look for as an owner.

When presented with an opportunity to take advantage of a situation, how honest are we? Try this one on for size: You're in a store waiting by the counter to buy something and no one is around. You notice the cash drawer is open about 1/4 inch. Do you reach in and grab the money? Probably not. But let's just say you walk up to the cash register, you find yourself alone and there is a $100 bill on the floor. Do you pick it up and pocket it or look for its owner? Hmmmm? Or for the third scenario, the cashier's station is closing as you walk up. The cashier is taking the cash drawer out of the register and walking away. You notice a $100 bill sitting on the counter by the register. Do you flag down the cashier and tell him, or do you pocket it?

You might have said yes to all, no to all, or made a split decision, depending on what you think is morally acceptable. My point here is that I believe most people are honest. It's my job as a boss to keep those honest people honest and not provide situations that would allow them to test their morality.

The Boardwalk Restaurant was an open playbook when it came to scams, with corruption going on in every department. One of my favorites was what I called "the big brunch scam." This involved dropping the same check over and over on different tables. Brunch was always busy. We had a real nice setup: a waffle station with eight irons, omelet station with ten hot chafing dishes, eight different salads, danish, bagels, fruit, yogurt, a carving station and dessert bar, plus the best ocean views on Long Island.

The buffet was around $12 and drinks were included, so the checks were always the same for the same number of guests: two guests are $24, four guests, $48. The scam was dropping the same check over and over, all day. If a couple paid cash, the server would pocket the cash and drop the same check at the next deuce that sat in their section, and so on.

I was just as guilty of working the system as the waitstaff. My particular scam went beyond the doors of the Boardwalk Restaurant. I had become friendly with a customer and through conversation found out that he was an usher at Shea Stadium, the home of the New York Mets. So Eddie and I started attending Met games, sitting in Tony's section on field level right above the dugout. We had the pleasure of meeting two New York City Mayors seated near us on opening days over the years, Ed Koch and David Dinkins…and by coincidence, Tony and his wife enjoyed complimentary brunch every Sunday at the Boardwalk.

Another doozy of a scam, more creative in my opinion, but not as lucrative as dropping the same check over and over, was the "Buy one get one free of equal or lesser value" scam. A table comes in for lunch, orders fish and chips and a burger, and hands in the coupon with the cash. The waiter pockets the coupon and uses his own money to pay for the free meal. Then during the dinner shift when another table orders for example, lobster tails and a seafood platter, he staples the coupon to that check and pockets the cash for the more expensive entrée. Pretty sweet!

The corporation that held the contract for the Jones Beach Foodservice was sold or merged several times in the years I worked there. Every other year or so, I got a new set of bosses and was taught a new set of ways to do the same job I had already been doing. We used to laugh about it, but looking back I was very lucky to have been able to work under so many different people in such a short amount of time. It was a tremendous experience—one I could write a whole other book about.

The basement of the restaurant housed the stewards, and the stewards controlled the restaurant. They managed food, liquor and dry good storage, and the distribution of those goods. Among them were my two friends Rich L. (not my partner Rich) and Eddie, who along with another, kept the flow of goods running smoothly. They also made sure our whiffle ball field in the middle of the main storeroom was kept free of any annoying things like dry goods that could get in the way of a game.

When I did my CIA externship at The Boardwalk Restaurant, the menu had an outdated '70s style and feel, including shell steak served with a baked potato, baked or fried fish sprinkled with breadcrumbs and a piece of broccoli, half a broiled chicken, and liver and onions. I'd like to segue into soda for a second before we get into the liver story.

Soda, in restaurants, comes from a gun or fountain, unlike the soda you buy at a store in a bottle or can. Modern restaurants buy boxes of syrup and pressurized tanks of CO_2 to carbonate the soda on premises. This saves on storage space and money since you don't have to pay the shipping costs for the water. The CO_2 tanks were stored in the basement and were overseen by the stewards. We used the CO_2 for three things: soda, cleaning refrigeration coils and the liver.

While most of the tanks were chained up on the loading dock and linked directly to the soda system, one was set aside and outfitted with a hose and spray nozzle. We used the high pressure air to blow out dust from the refrigeration coils, similar to the can of air you buy at Staples to blow dust, dandruff, potato chips and fingernail clippings out of your keyboard, only much larger.

Calves' liver was delivered fresh weekly and was pink in color. It would be portioned into 10-ounce steaks and sent upstairs to the cooking line. The scrap pieces would be cubed for ourselves and sautéed medium rare with some mushrooms, onions, Madeira wine and demi-glace and served over pasta for our lunch. It was absolutely delicious.

If it happened to rain a few days in a row and business was slow, combined with some improper inventory rotation, the unsold liver started to turn green. It was then sent back downstairs and that's where the magic happened.

Rich or Eddie would rinse off the liver, dry it and lay it out on a sheet pan, then take the spare tank of CO_2 that we used for cleaning refrigerator coils and spray it on the liver. The CO_2 instantly changed the color of the liver from green back into a nice shade of pink. It was then wrapped and sent back up to the line for service. You think that's gross, right? Yeah, it is! But we're kids just following orders. "Ours was not to question why. Ours was just to sauté and fry." So we kept our mouths shut.

Everyone has had one of those moments when they see something and say, "I was doing that years ago. If I had brought that to market, I would have become a millionaire." Well, guess what? It really happened and we could have become millionaires. If you've ever had sushi and ordered the Ahi tuna, there's a good chance it was sprayed with CO_2. Next time you order some, notice the pinkish red color of your tuna. It's that color because it was processed and sprayed with CO_2 just like we used to do with the liver. It's not to change spoiled fish to fresh; it's done to maintain its appearance.

Fresh caught tuna is brownish red, not pinkish red. Some genius smarter than me realized that he could spray the brown tuna with gas, turn it a more appetizing reddish pink color and sell it as Ahi tuna. If you order a Bluefin or fresh caught tuna at your local sushi joint, you'll notice the color difference right away.

Some of our stewards were also rounds men, acting in the restaurant the way a utility player does on a baseball team. They weren't the best, but in a pinch they could fill any position when the first string man was out. This is not normal in the industry and we were very lucky to have guys like this: they filled in as prep men, line cooks, and expeditors and they were occasionally selected for what we referred to as "Special Assignment," which was any job that was outside the confines of the restaurant.

One particular night our sauté cook banged in sick and Eddie got the call to work at the sauté station, one of the busiest and most prestigious spots on the cooking line. No one starts off on sauté; it's a position you work up to. Our sauté station had only five menu items all cooked or "ala minute" or made to order, but it was responsible for about 150 covers on a busy night (a cover is restaurant lingo for how many customers you serve in a meal period).

The story goes that in the old grandiose turn-of-the-century hotels, as the kitchen plated up the entrées, the waiters would put metal covers on top of the plates to keep the food warm on the journey from kitchen to dining room. They still do today in most catering halls, stacking them as high as they can to save on trips to the dining room. At the end of the night, when they wanted to know how busy they were, they would count the dirty plate covers that came back into the kitchen to determine how many meals they served. Hence the term.

Theoretically, the sauté cook preparing 150 meals would be cooking the same five dishes individually 30 times per night. Sauté was not an easy job to do and as I said, it also is considered the lead station and one of prestige as far as the kitchen goes. That is, until Eddie got there.

Eddie was a sharp-minded kid destined for law school who figured there had to be an easier way than cooking 150 meals individually. He decided to take out all the shelving in his refrigerator on the cooking line and fill it from floor to ceiling with every single 14-, 18-, 24- and 36-inch sauté pan we had, pre-loaded with all the ingredients for each of his dishes.

Talk about *mise en place*! For a guy who had hardly worked a day on the sauté station and had little guidance, I had to give him credit. When the expeditor would call out and order for chicken and broccoli, Eddie would grab a pan with 4 or 5 orders pre-loaded in it and throw it on the fire, then he could sit back and relax as the next few orders came in. Eddie had turned the concept of cooking to order to that of serving off a buffet line at a soup kitchen. This ended up being the last time Eddie worked the sauté station and the first of many lasts for Eddie.

I gave him credit for his out-of-the-box thinking and problem-solving skills. He was also working on another project that never came to fruition, The Premade Reuben Sandwich. He had been experimenting by assembling the sandwich, freezing it and dropping it into in the fryer to speed up lunch service, but it never really worked. I have to say, though, he was about 30 years ahead of his time, as today many sandwiches and entrées at chain restaurants are made very similarly to the way Eddie designed his Premade Reuben but with modern-day technology.

TurboChef is a company that makes combi ovens, which are souped-up versions of commercial-grade combination microwave/convection ovens, the perfect piece of equipment for Eddie's sandwiches. Instead of dropping them in the fryer, today all a modern-day line cook has to do is take the premade sandwich out of the freezer, brush the bread with butter, and put it in the combi oven for 45 seconds. Out comes a perfectly grilled Reuben. More restaurants than you realize are taking advantage of this technology to save on labor costs and speed up service. It's not for all applications, but if a quality product goes into the combi oven, a quality product comes out of it.

Another one of Eddie's lasts occurred on Easter Sunday, when he was selected for a highly coveted Special Assignment. The sous chef at the time was a great guy, nicknamed Shang. Shang's full name was Hooshang Nemetelahi. He and his brother, Farhang, had immigrated to America from Iran, but since Iran had somewhat recently taken 52 Americans hostage and held them for over a year, he felt it was better to say he was from Persia. Persia hadn't existed for well over a thousand years, but not once did anyone besides me question him on it.

Here it was, Easter Sunday and the restaurant, as usual, was overflowing with reservations. It was a beautiful, sunny, spring day with families dressed in their Sunday best, strolling along the boardwalk. The powers that be had rented a bunny suit and, wouldn't you know it, it was just Eddie's size, so it was decided Eddie would be the perfect man for the Easter Bunny gig.

Despite several suggestions by us that he might not be the best choice, management felt that since his height and body size fit the suit best, he was the man for the job. We suited him up, gave him his basket of eggs and sent him out onto the boardwalk to entertain the kids. Not five minutes later, he walked back into the restaurant, covered in dripping egg yolks with several sets of irate parents trailing behind him, screaming bloody murder.

Hooshang, being from Persia or wherever, didn't fully grasp the concept of the Easter Egg and had dyed a bunch of soft-boiled eggs. No one is really sure exactly how it went down on the boardwalk. There are conflicting stories, but it seems some of the nastier kids were clearly not happy with soft-boiled eggs breaking in their hands and started throwing them at each other, then back at Eddie. Eddie, not happy with getting hit with the eggs, grabbed one of the kids and said rather loudly in front of the parents, "Listen, kid, me and Santa are really close and you ain't getting shit for Christmas." Needless to say, several families enjoyed free brunch that afternoon and we all had a great laugh, celebrating the first and last day of Eddie's public relations career.

OVERCOOKED

Ivan Sayles

Chapter Thirty-one

My Addiction II

The statistical rate of success in recovering permanently from crack cocaine is less than 5 percent.
—U.S. DEPARTMENT OF HEALTH AND HUMAN SERVICES

Ninety-five out of every hundred crack addicts will never overcome their addiction. They will die on the streets or end up in jail. For the remainder of my life, I will be a drug addict. I will be a drug addict when I walk Amanda down the aisle. I will be a drug addict when I hold my first grandchild. And I will be a drug addict the day they put me in the ground. The question is, what will I make of my addiction? Have I been cursed by it or blessed by it?

Winston Churchill said, "A pessimist sees the difficulty in every opportunity; an optimist sees opportunity in every difficulty." Is it not inspiring when you see a person either having developed or been born with a disability rise to do something extraordinary? Take Jim Abbott, for example. Not familiar with Mr. Abbott? He was a Major League Baseball pitcher for the New York Yankees, who was born with one hand. As if it weren't amazing enough that he made it to the Major Leagues, on September 4, 1993, he pitched a no-hitter. A no-hitter! He pitched one of only 272 no-hitters in the entire history of Major League Baseball at that time.

Considering there are 4,860 games in a season in modern-day baseball, and the first official no-hitter was pitched 144 years ago by George Bradley in 1876, that's quite an accomplishment. Jim Abbott had to practice longer and work harder than anyone else to accomplish what he did. So my question is, in the case of baseball, was he blessed or cursed by having only one hand? Would he have accomplished what he did, had he been born with two hands and not been forced to work so hard?

The combination of having an addiction and the strong desire to overcome it can drive one to accomplish incredible things, to appreciate life with a clarity, sharpness, and perception that those without the disability may never see. This was the epiphany of overcoming my addiction, getting that proverbial monkey off my back, an expression I never fully understood until I became clean. The monkey was an omnipresent weight that consumed me and dragged me into a bottomless pit of oblivion, but thankfully the pit had an escape tunnel.

Recovery wasn't easy and it didn't happen overnight. It took five arrests, a failed intervention, three different rehab programs and more relapses than I can remember. It also took me two years from the day I decided to get clean until I finally did it, but I never gave up. The sad truth of my predicament is that neither I, nor anyone else, can say if my recovery was successful. Not until I'm in the ground anyway, when my loved ones can look back and say he never used again.

Early in my recovery, I began going to AA (Alcoholics Anonymous) and NA (Narcotics Anonymous) meetings. The two are very similar, but I started leaning toward the AA meetings vs. the NA meetings. In the beginning it was simply because the AA meetings were half an hour shorter, but as time went on I found I just liked AA better. From my best guesstimate, about half of the people in AA were also addicted to drugs, so I fit right in. I came to realize it really didn't matter whether it was drugs, alcohol, gambling or any other addiction, as the symptoms of the disease of addiction, no matter what strain you have, are all the same.

I experimented with various meetings around town, trying to find the ones that fit me best. I had no idea there were so many near me. It's kind of like when you buy a new car, and then all of a sudden everywhere you look, you see the same car. Once I knew what I was looking for, I couldn't miss them.

Scattered within four miles of my house were meetings almost every hour of every day, from 7 a.m. to 10 p.m. There was even a 7 a.m. "early risers" meeting at Jones Beach on Sundays. At first, as I made my way around the rooms, I'd just hang around and listen to people talk. As I started seeing familiar faces, I became more comfortable, engaging in conversation and even speaking, or "sharing," as it's called. Each of the different rooms had its own particular vibe. Within a few weeks, I found my niche and the particular meetings I liked.

It's pretty much the same as you've seen on television or in movies. Visualize if you will, the portion of the meeting where a person such as me would stand up and say, "Hi. My name is Ivan, and I'm a drug addict." Then the crowd responds, "Hi, Ivan," and then Ivan begins to tell his story. In real life, that's pretty much how it goes.

Some people tell stories of addiction and each story is as unique as the individual telling it, while others just say what they are feeling at the moment. There are no rules. Often there is a "guest speaker," someone who has been in the program for a while, celebrating a milestone in his or her sobriety.

As I listened to the stories over many months, throughout the different rooms, I realized the characters and scenery would change, but the plot was always the same. Every story contained a common ground I could relate to, so I felt a sense of belonging, a sense of family. Most stories, or at least the ones I related to, were of a once-beautiful, loving human being metamorphosing into a greedy, self-serving monster, who would sacrifice everything for the sake of a drink. Once I became comfortable I began to speak, which ultimately led to my writing this book.

It was liberating for me to stand in front of a group of my peers, most of them strangers, and share my darkest secrets—confessing the worst of my sins, and speaking of the horrors I had done to myself and to the people I loved all with the reassurance of knowing I would not be judged.

One could be clean for two months, relapse for weeks, start day one of their sobriety again for the tenth time and be welcomed with open arms. Take it one day at a time, they said. Don't worry about tomorrow, as long as you're clean today. This was very significant to my recovery. Relapse is part of recovery, they said. I haven't met anyone yet who has just decided one day to stop and never use again. As one gentleman used to say in the meetings, "It took me eight years to get one year sober." I'm grateful that it took less time for me.

After every relapse, I'd feel ashamed and depressed. My mind was on recovery, but my actions did not coincide. Having to tell my friends and family that I relapsed was mortifying, so of course I lied. They would see my progress and encourage me, but when I slipped, I felt I was judged. Perhaps it was just my guilt. I knew what I had done. Getting reprimanded for it or looked down upon by my friends and family did not help me, it just drove me further away.

The best thing you can do for addicts when they slip is help them up, dust them off and point them back in the right direction. Nothing more, nothing less! Whatever you do, don't put too much effort into it. If they slip again, which they probably will, you may feel slighted or burned, but don't think about it. If you do, you won't have the open mind you need in order to deal with and help the addict.

Don't get personal or emotional, and remember you have absolutely no control over an addict's actions. The only one who can keep an addict clean is the addict himself. It wasn't until I found these AA rooms, filled with wonderful people afflicted with the same sickness as mine, with their anonymity and non-judgmental nature, that I began to be able to open my mind and realize what my disease was all about.

As time went on, I noticed some people, when speaking to the room, would begin by saying, "Hi. I'm so and so. I'm a grateful alcoholic or grateful drug addict." That blew me away. I didn't understand: a grateful addict? Grateful for what? How could anyone be grateful for an addiction? Bear in mind that at that point in my life I was one step above skid row. Years of addiction had done plenty of mental and physical damage to my body. I'd lost several years of my life to a glass pipe and was struggling to regain the trust of family and friends—not full trust, but the beginnings of trust. The basic trust that is handed out so freely to mere strangers every day.

What did I have to be grateful about? I didn't understand. I'd been cursed with this addiction, this cancer that was consuming me from the inside out. It had spread throughout my body, destroying everything that was once human inside me. It tore my family apart, while they helplessly watched me wither away. I was battling for recovery and relapsing along the way. How could I be grateful for something like that?

Like most addicts, I had become bitter and spiteful, pissed off at myself and blaming everyone else for my problems. Over time, that changed and I became one of those addicts who was truly grateful. I am grateful for my inner strength, which enabled me to conquer my foe. Grateful for the way my recovery has allowed me to appreciate every breath I take.

I had been sniffing cocaine for most of my adulthood, and although I didn't realize it until I began to walk down the path to recovery, I was a functioning addict. I was one of so many out there, able to juggle their addictions with their everyday lives. People with families, cars, and white picket fences, who show up on time for work and perform their daily tasks adequately…you can spot them easily if you know what to look for. They'll have bags under their eyes, are a little cranky, and most probably have a very short fuse.

They might blame it on a rough night out and laugh it off with co-workers as just another day in the life—the party guy in the office and the last one to go home for the night. That was me. I plowed through my days, went through the motions at half-speed and everyone accepted me for who I was. I showed up at my family functions. I went about the routines, never reaching more than 50 percent of my potential, keeping my drug habits just under the radar.

I was a party guy, and no one wanted to confront me on my recreational drug use as long as I kept the status quo. The king was standing naked in the room. It wasn't until my addiction took over that my life came grinding to a halt. I went from operating at 50 percent to zero in an instant when I started smoking crack every day, forsaking my family and friends for drugs, contacting them only in attempts to extract favors or borrow money.

It wasn't until I hit rock bottom, until I hit zero, that I finally realized the 100 percent I could become. For 20 years I'd been operating at half-speed in a losing battle of trying to balance my life with my drug use. I was now a full-blown junkie.

So now, I am grateful for my addiction. It's made me the man I am today. Sometimes I feel it was my destiny, the road that was mapped out for me at birth. I certainly wouldn't be in the relationship I'm in today without my addiction. Why? I would have taken Jen for granted and fucked it up, like every relationship before her, putting myself and my own selfish needs before anyone else.

Working so hard to overcome my addiction has given me the strength and drive to overcome any obstacles thrown my way. It has taught me that nothing worthwhile comes without determination and sacrifice. Addiction may have been the path I needed to take, outlined for me by a power greater than myself. Without it I would never have reached rock bottom. Zero was what I needed in order to realize I could attain infinity, to learn there is no limit to my potential.

Ivan Sayles

Chapter Thirty-two

Rules and Regulations

C o-mingling with other humans would not be possible without rules and regulations. Some rules don't have much wiggle room, like murder for example, while others do, like gliding through a stop sign.

Same is true for my company. When we first opened 23 years ago, I didn't have an employee manual. Eighteen years ago we had one about five pages long, and now we have one half the size of this book and employees are required to take an online program on sexual harassment. It's grown over the years, mostly from experience: Ivan gets screwed in some way, shape or form, and the rule book enlarges.

It usually goes something like this: Drinking at the bar after your shift is allowed at Rachel's, as long as you're not in uniform and you have management permission. One of our waitresses had just gotten off her shift. She had recently gotten engaged and was sitting next to the service area where the staff picks up drinks from the bar, having a cocktail. As I was walking through the dining room, a table called me over, inquiring as to the status of their meal. They'd been waiting a long time. I asked them to hold on...I'd look into it right away.

I took a quick scan in the dining room and didn't see the server, so I headed into the kitchen to see what was going on. "How are we looking on table four?" I yelled to the middleman.

The middleman is the person in charge of the cooking line when we don't have an expediter. It's a chain of command kind of thing, where the front of the house staff only speaks to one person in the kitchen and that person speaks to everyone else.

We also refer to this person or any employee given a task of responsibility who is in charge of a certain aspect of things, as the "POOR" person, an acronym I came up with, meaning "Person of organization and responsibility," which is very appropriate, because that poor sap has to answer to me if something gets screwed up. The middleman pointed to the four dishes under the heat lamp and said, "It's sitting right there."

I'd covered the kitchen and the dining room, so I checked the bar. As I approached her, I saw the waitress who had just gotten engaged, with her arm stretched out, open palmed like a traffic cop proudly halting a speeding cement truck, and my google-eyed server admiring the rock on her ring finger, while the bread on table four's steak sandwich was turning to toast under the heat lamp.

I probably shouldn't go into what I actually said to them, but I can say the rulebook changed that day. Don't worry, employees are still allowed to have a drink at the bar with permission. I'm not that much of a prick, but they are no longer allowed to sit within three stools of the service area and are not allowed to talk to employees who are working.

Among our rules, there are some zero-tolerance ones. Here are my top two:

Never, under any circumstances, is a server allowed to question a customer about a tip.

No cell phones.

Cell phones anywhere in a workplace, specifically a customer service area, pisses me off. Guy walks into a bar...sounds like a joke, right? It's not....and the bartender, on her cell phone, raises her hand with index finger pointed up and mouths, "I'll be right with you" or at the counter or the customer service desk or wherever.

My cell phone rule did not start as zero tolerance but rather grew over time. At first servers were allowed to have them on their person as long as they were on silent or vibrate. It wasn't until I heard a phone ringing in a server's apron at a table while taking a customer's order that cell phones were no longer allowed on their person. These days, just seeing a cell phone in the hand of an employee who's not on break, is cause for a reprimand. By some strange coincidence, however, my staff seems to have to pee a lot more than they used to. But whatever—out of sight, out of mind, right?

I've been fortunate to have a community that supports my restaurant, so giving back just seems to be the natural order of things, and helping those less fortunate than myself has become very important to me. I firmly believe that I have been blessed with success and owe it to myself to pay it forward.

We make donations to pretty much any local organization that asks. I volunteer my time and sit on the board of directors of a school for kids with social, emotional, and behavioral disorders.

One of the ways we as a restaurant help those less fortunate is through "tastings." This happens to be one of my favorite forms of charity. Tastings are fundraisers where restaurants, wineries, markets and the like set up tables and offer free samples of their products. The vendors do the event for free and in exchange, get to chit chat, promote and sample their product to potential customers, usually accompanied by a DJ or live music. The charity sells the tickets to raise money for its cause and the guests have an enjoyable night out sampling wines and food from all over Long Island. It's a win-win for everyone!

We had a tasting scheduled and I thought it might be fun to do it with Jen. That particular event was actually not a charity function, but a launch party for a new product made by Sail Away Coffee, or as we on Long Island say, cawffee. Sail Away is a local cold brew coffee company, whose product we carry, modify with whiskey, Kahlua and whipped cream and sell as an Iced

OVERCOOKED

Irish Coffee. If you enjoy liquor and coffee, you have to try one of our Iced Irish!

The tasting was on the second floor of some artsy-fartsy gallery in East Rockaway, attended predominantly by what Rich lovingly refers to as, "A bunch of tattooed, microbrew-drinking, soy-eating vegan beardtards." Not that there's anything wrong with that. After all, as a modern-day restaurant, we do cater to the general public and have menu selections geared toward millennials. I hope I covered my partner's ass on that one, but probably not.

East Rockaway, being on the south shore of Long Island, is prone to periodic flooding under the right conditions. Specifically, a strong southwesterly wind, combined with a full moon, will produce high waters in low-lying coastal residential areas. This was happening on the night of the Sail Away tasting. The south shore of Long Island was under a flood watch that evening, so after we set up and started serving, I decided to go downstairs and check out the water level in the street, lest we get trapped in East Rockaway for hours until the tide went out.

I told Jen to hold down the fort; I would be back in a few. The place was starting to get crowded and as I made my way up front, I saw people were jammed on the stairway coming in, waiting to pay or register at the front desk. I noticed an exit sign behind the DJ booth at the back of the room, so I decided to use that exit rather than fight the crowd.

I opened the steel door and walked down the flight of stairs, only to find the exit blocked by a pallet stacked with boxes. I shook my head. Just my luck. I took a picture of the pile blocking the door with my phone and sent it to Rich, jokingly captioned with "Look at this shit! You know if it had been us, we would have gotten a $10,000 fine from the fire marshal for blocking an emergency exit!"

As I walked back up the stairs, the joke was on me. There was no handle on the inside of the door at the top. FUCK! I'm not a claustrophobic person, but after a few minutes of screaming and pounding on the door, I have to admit it was starting to get a little stuffy in that stairwell. I must have called Jen at least 20 times and got no answer. I really wasn't looking forward to spending the next hour or so trapped in the stairwell.

I continued blowing up Jen's phone, wondering what the heck she could be doing and why she wasn't answering. After about 25 minutes or so, I finally timed my screaming and pounding just right in between songs and DJ the heard me and opened the door. I believe I actually gasped for breath as I bolted out of the stairwell. Sometimes, I can be a real pussy.

When I got back to the table, Jen was doing her thing, passing out samples, smiling and chatting with the guests. She made some sort of where the fuck have you been? type comment. I just smiled and asked, "Jen, by the way, where is your cell phone?" She straightened up, literally snapping to attention, and proudly proclaimed, "It's in my pocketbook, on silent. I know how strict you are about cell phones at work!"

OVERCOOKED

Chapter Thirty-three

My Near-Gay Experience

At the turn of the century, my life was pretty good. I'd purchased my parents' house, was single, owned two restaurants and was making decent money. I began hanging out at a Cajun restaurant called the Bayou in North Bellmore. The Bayou was a single-storefront, authentic Cajun restaurant with maybe 40 seats and a 14-stool bar. It was the only one of its kind in our area and let me tell you, they packed them in.

One of their ex-chefs, Billy, came to work for Rachel's and put a Cajun influence on our menu. He started our annual Mardis Gras menu and Fat Tuesday party, which became the influence for the opening of our New Orleans–style restaurant, NAWLINS, right next door to RACHEL'S. Billy still plays the drums to this day in the Zydeco band at our annual Fat Tuesday Party some 20 years later.

The Bayou was located in a strip mall with a purple sign barely visible from the road across the parking lot. A bumper sticker with their slogan "Big Fun" was plastered on the wooden front door. They definitely beat to their own drum, they didn't serve lunch, they kept the door locked until 5 p.m. and customers would line up outside waiting for them to open. When you walked in from the sunlight, you'd be blind for a second as your eyes tried to adjust to the darkness of the interior, while your senses were assaulted with the glorious smells of an authentic Louisiana kitchen and sounds of Zydeco and jazz.

As your sight gradually adjusted to the darkness, Mardi Gras beads of purple and gold hanging everywhere would come into focus. New Orleans memorabilia including posters of Etta James and Louis Armstrong hung near purple string lights that were the only source of illuminating the interior of the restaurant. You were no longer on Long Island in the CVS shopping center, you were in NOLA on Decatur.

The menu was limited, with only five or six entrees, and kids were persona non grata. This was an adult playground. I think their customer service policy was: this is the way we do it. If you don't like it, don't let the door hit you on the ass on the way out. Customers are like buses. Another one will come along in 15 minutes. It worked for them.

As soon as the door opened, the place was five deep at the bar with people waiting to sit down and eat. Somehow, they also managed to squeeze in a band. The owners were gay and so were many of their employees. To use the Seinfeld cliché, "Not that there's anything wrong with that," and there isn't. The only reason I mention it is because it's relevant to this particular story.

I had become friendly with the owners and had gotten to know many of the employees. It wasn't until a cute little red-headed bartender named Jen (different Jen) caught my eye that I really started hanging out there. Several nights a week after closing up the Smithville Café, I would head over for a few drinks, a late-night bite and some cocaine. Go figure.

It was January of 2001 and lo and behold, my beloved Giants were in the Super Bowl. I was invited to Manhattan with the Bayou crew to watch the game and since Jen was going, so was I. We checked into the hotel with two sets of adjoining rooms. After we settled in we all met downstairs at the bar to watch the Giants get crushed by Baltimore. We went back up to the room for a few lines of coke and off to the Limelight. At the Limelight, I drank, sniffed coke, and danced—and as if that wasn't enough, someone broke out some ecstasy. Well, why the fuck not? This was a party, right? Not sure how we all made it back to the hotel, but we did.

Best I can recall, I was sitting on the bed under the covers with Jen, the two of us drinking beer, high as a kite. There were several other people in the room and three or four others sitting on the bed, among them a very effeminate black man in his mid-20s who worked for a local entertainment company whose name I've forgotten. His job was to go to weddings, sweet sixteens and other events, to assist the emcee in getting the crowd fired up, which seems to me like a gateway job that might lead to a promising career as a fluffer, but what the hell do I know?

Picture a young Eddie Murphy impersonating Nathan Lane's character Albert in Bird Cage and you'll get the idea. Anyway, Jen was to my right bullshitting with everyone, and Prince Albert was sitting on the edge of the bed to my left. As I looked over at her, I saw she was holding a beer in her right hand, talking and smiling, and then I felt her hand running up my leg. I gave Jen a knowing smile and she smiled back and continued to talk to me and the people on her side of the bed as my cock was being stroked into an erection. I found myself very impressed with Jen.

She didn't miss a beat. She just kept talking, business as usual, engaging other people in the room while stroking my cock. This was hot; the thrill of her doing this without anyone knowing was really turning me on. As Jen turned to me, I gave her a knowing wink and as she winked back at me, she pulled her left hand from under the cover and scratched her head. High as I was, it took me a second or two to figure out something wasn't right. If Jen had a beer in her right hand and was scratching her head with the left, then whose hand was stroking my cock?

You know it! As I turned my head away from Jen, I saw Prince Albert with a big shit-eating grin on his face. I said to him ever so discreetly, "Get your fucking hand off my dick and move away from the bed." He crooned, "Come on, Ivan; let me suck your dick. You know it'll feel good." I wasn't having any part of that and made it abundantly clear by taking my left foot and kicking his ass off the bed. So, my friend, my advice to you is: Next time you find a hand stroking your cock under the covers, it's a good idea to find out whose arm it belongs to!

Ivan Sayles

Chapter Thirty-four

I Must Have Fallen Asleep in My Sandwich

With my stint in New England done and my Stone Catering experience behind me, I returned to the Boardwalk Restaurant as a sous chef (assistant chef). I was 20 years old, skinny, had a full head of hair and the world in front of me. It's during those next few years that I forged the bonds of friendship between my partner Rich, better known as "Rockhead" at the time, and my best friend, Eddie. We maintain that friendship today, some 35 years later, a bond I have no doubt will continue for the rest of our lives.

The kitchen at the Boardwalk ran the length of the dining room, which sat 450 people. The length is roughly half the length of a football field with the dishwashing machine, pot-sinks and cashier's booth at the west end, and office, service bar, stairs and elevator at the east end. Stairs and an elevator lead down to the loading dock and eight walk-in refrigerators, freezers, lockers, showers, soda, liquor, boiler, dry storage and locker rooms. Upstairs we had five walk-in refrigerators and a prep area that ran parallel behind the hot side with three large steam kettles, sinks, prep tables, steamers, a mixing machine, slicer and buffalo chopper. Rich worked the pantry station "cold side." This is where we prepared all the à la carte or made-to-order sandwiches and salads. It was located directly across from, and ran parallel to, the "hot side," where all the à la carte hot cooking was done. Genius! This is where I, and sometimes Eddie, worked.

Eddie was a steward, line cook, dishwasher or expediter, depending on what was needed on that particular day. His primary job was stewarding, which basically consisted of receiving, stocking and distributing products throughout the restaurant. I mostly expedited, made soups and sauces, and dealt with problems typical to being second in command of a 450-seat restaurant.

Our 20-year-old selves worked hard all day and partied harder all night. After work, groups of eight to ten of us would go out to Perry's Place, now called Snaps, The Wantagh Inn, Mulcahy's or the Peacock Lounge (which has since closed), all within walking distance of each other. Our favorite bartender from the Peacock Lounge ended up opening his own place, Mr. Berry's, in Bethpage, New York, which he still runs today.

Steve had his moment in the spotlight, hosting rallies and spearheading the movement against the brutality of making smokers stand outside to smoke in Nassau County. He enjoyed a short-lived victory until about a year later, in 2003, when NY State outlawed all smoking indoors, followed by the rest of the nation shortly thereafter. These digs were all located within walking distance of each other in a one-block radius, conveniently just two exits north of Jones Beach off the Wantagh Parkway.

Let me digress into an explanation of the term parkway. If you're not from Long Island or the surrounding area, this is a unique feature of our roadways and has caused many a Long Islander to ponder the question, "Why do we park in our driveways and drive on our parkways?"

Our system of roadways all have parks at the end of them, which is probably why they're called parkways. Well, all except the Northern State Parkway. They were designed in the 1920s by an alleged racist and public official named Robert Moses, nicknamed "The Master Builder." The parkways were designed for passenger cars only. Robert Moses did this to prevent buses from the city from driving on them and bringing the "lower classes" out to Long Island. Only people affluent enough to own cars were worthy of enjoying his roads and the parks and beaches they led to.

To ensure this would forever be the case, he designed beautiful, sturdy stone-faced bridges that still stand today, too low to accommodate buses…or, as it turns out, modern-day tractor-trailers. No commercial vehicles are allowed on Long Island parkways. Local bus and truck drivers know to stay off our parkways; out-of-town tractor-trailer drivers, however, do not. These drivers sometimes fall victim to the curse of The Master Builder because they are not privy to this information or they fail to read local road signs. Several times a year, trucks run into the beautiful and remarkably strong stone bridges that Robert Moses built.

At 50 to 60 miles per hour, the forward inertia would sometimes push the entire tractor and trailer combo under the bridge and out the other side. Once through, the trailer looks like someone took the roof off with a giant can opener that just couldn't quite catch its grip, peeling the top off the trailer in jagged ten-foot sections.

I've only seen one of these in real-time and it was pretty intense. The other five or six I've witnessed were after the fact, with a bewildered driver standing on the side of the road, surrounded by what seemed to be every state trooper within a 50-mile radius, shaking his head in disbelief, while overlooking the accordion that was once his truck and receiving a shit-ton of summonses for his stupidity.

My former boss at the Boardwalk Restaurant, Michael, who now has two fabulous restaurants, FIRE AND WINE and VAI'S ITALIAN INSPIRED KITCHEN, right outside of Chicago, knew someone very well that hit one of our overpasses while driving a tanker truck, stopping traffic where it burned for two days before the fire department felt it was no longer at risk of exploding and was able to move in to extinguish the flames. Thankfully Roger walked away from the accident.

We would eat and drink at the bars five or six nights a week, partying 'til closing time at 4 a.m., going to bed for a few hours and starting all over the next day. I honestly don't know how we did it. Cooks slept with waitresses, bartenders slept with waitresses, lifeguards slept with waitresses, managers slept with waitresses, even some of the NY State Park Police slept with the waitresses. Anyone who wasn't sleeping with a waitress was in competition with someone to sleep with a waitress.

Don't get me wrong: it wasn't some giant orgy. There were plenty of serious relationships and some great marriages that resulted from those relationships, including my partner Rich and his wife, as well as friends Steve and Eric Ducey. I even got lucky enough over the six years I worked there to find two girls who said they would marry me but then later changed their minds. In retrospect, that was some damn good decision making on their part, considering what the next 23 years of my existence would be like.

As life is full of surprises, about four years ago, I became Facebook friends with engagement number two, Christina. After learning her son Ryan was interested in becoming a chef, Rich and I took him under our wing and hired him as a cook. Ryan fit right into our fun-loving, sarcastic family. Ryan did not live locally like most of our employees, and when asked how he came to work at NAWLINS, he would tell everyone "Because Ivan used to fuck my mom."

After Ryan worked at two of our locations and dated two of our waitresses, he decided he wanted to go to culinary school, attending my alma mater, the Culinary Institute of America. Ryan and I even started calling each other father and son, joking about what might have been had I married his mom. I still owe you a baseball game, son!

One particular Saturday night, I was out with the crew. It was the mid '80s, which means if you were in the hairspray or cocaine business you were making good money. I was no exception, subsidizing my cocaine habit by selling to friends. That night, we were at the Wantagh Inn and Rich was all decked out in an era-appropriate outfit consisting of Cavaricci parachute jeans (baggy at the thigh, tight at the ankles), paired with a sweet pair of alligator-skin boots, collarless white shirt and bolo tie.

Saturday night was always challenging for us because we kitchen folk had to be in at the crack of 8 a.m. to prepare for Sunday brunch. Considering bars in New York close at 4 a.m., Sunday morning was a who's who of green-faced young men and women doing their best not to throw up while scrambling eggs or mixing waffle batter, desperately trying to pull it all together before we opened at noon.

It was going on 3 a.m. After witnessing several shots go into Rich's mouth, followed by several lewd remarks coming out of his mouth concerning a particular waitress Rich felt he needed to tell what a sperm-burping whore she was, I decided to intervene before things got out of hand. As I put my arm around him and guided him away from the situation, I reminded him he was scheduled for brunch at 8 a.m. He said, "Just call me in the morning at 7:30 and wake me up."

Long before cell phones, we were still kids living with our parents, so calling him in the morning meant calling his house, not necessarily calling him. My parents, like many other families at the time, had only one phone in the entire house—a wall-mounted rotary-dial model. For you young 'uns, this meant you had to stick your finger into a dial and spin it one number at a time until you completed the seven- or ten-number sequence.

Phones were usually located in the kitchen, the handset tethered to the phone by a cord that was tangled up like a rat's nest. Some could stretch all the way to the back yard so the person on the phone could walk far enough away from the rest of the family to have some privacy while talking. It was not unheard of to find a family member, usually a sister, inside a closet with the door closed, speaking in the dark.

I inquired how my calling Rich's house on Sunday morning at 7:30 would sit with his parents. He replied, "My mom doesn't care...she's up anyway." Well, not so much! I hadn't met his parents yet, but I knew they owned a junkyard in Lindenhurst. I wasn't sure if that's where Rich got his nickname "Rockhead" from, but it seemed very likely it could have been from "The Yard."

At 7:30, I called Rockhead's house, as instructed. His mom answered the phone in her most polite, Sunday morning, Scotch-drinking, cigarette-smoking, raspy, fuck-you, you-just-woke-me-up kind of voice. "Hello?" "Hi, um, good morning! Um... Mrs. Venticinque, it's me, um, Ivan from The Beach. Is Rich available?" It was silent for a second as she drew a long, deep breath and roared, "Riiiiiiich! Get the fuck out of bed! It's work! You're late! You'd better get your ass in there right now!"

I didn't even thank her or say goodbye. I just let the receiver slip away from my face, down my arm and back onto the cradle...fearful for my life, that I might meet this woman one day and she would remember I was the one who woke her that Sunday morning.

Twenty minutes later, Rich strolled into my office, his hair sticking straight up, wearing the same clothes from the night before. All the creases and starch were gone from his outfit, and he looked as though he had slept in his laundry bin. We went over the brunch prep work and as he turned to leave, I saw this greasy, lumpy, blotch on his back shoulder. "Rich, what is that on your back?" He turned his head as he pulled on his shirtsleeve to twist the back of his shirt around to see what I was talking about, and replied nonchalantly, "Oh, I must have fallen asleep in my sandwich." He did an about face and walked out of my office.

Ivan Sayles

Chapter Thirty-five

Really Good Bad Luck

Luck is a crazy thing and luck seems to come to different people in different ways, like life seems to come so easily to some people and is so difficult for others. Some people are lucky at gambling, some have great business luck, some athletes seem to always be involved in the big plays no matter where on the field they take place, or as Rod Stewart claims, "Some guys get all the breaks."

Me, not so much. Call it skill, education, training, confidence or instinct; I believe there is a certain amount of God-given luck unique to each person. Finding that luck within and exploiting it to maximize one's potential is up to the individual. I'll never win lotto. I'll never buy the winning box in a Super Bowl pool or pull on the arm on a slot machine and walk out of a casino $5 million richer, but that doesn't stop me from trying occasionally. After all, you gotta be in it to win it, right?

So, I buy a scratch-off or a Powerball ticket every once in a while, just to test the water to see if anything has changed, but so far nothing. My luck is different. They say cats have nine lives: then I must have twenty. I have escaped death by the skin of my teeth too many times. Is a guardian angel looking over my shoulder? Or am I destined for something that hasn't happened yet? Who knows?

OVERCOOKED

I have a friend, Gary, now a happily retired New York City firefighter, who has financial luck. By that I mean gambling luck: he always seems to be winning something. One year I thought some of his luck might have rubbed off on me, but I was wrong.

Firefighters have the ability to manipulate their work schedules by trading shifts with one another in a system called mutuals. Theoretically, you can work your full workweek in about a day and a half, working 24 hours a day and then have five and a half days off a week. In Gary's firehouse, there was a football pool where each firefighter "bought" a box by putting up one day of work as a bet instead of cash. It was a winner-take-all pool and Gary won. One hundred days off with pay! That's almost six months' paid vacation while all your buddies from work have to fill in your shifts. Oh, and he won $15,000 in another football pool at a local bar!

That same year, what happened to me? While I was on vacation in Puerto Rico, my cell phone rang. The call was from one of the owners of Jackie Reilly's, a popular Irish Pub, where I had purchased a $100 football box. I couldn't imagine why Sean was calling me on Super Bowl Sunday, one of his busiest days of the year, until he told me I won ten grand in the football pool. Now there's some good news!

Had I been anywhere else but an all-inclusive resort, this story might have ended badly for me, as I'm sure we would have blown through a considerable amount of cash that night celebrating my windfall. The next morning Sean called me back to tell me in his Irish brogue, "Em, Ouyvan, da ting is, I made a mistake. It was anouthour Ouyvan dat won de pool." Another fucking Ivan won the pool? In my entire lifetime I've only met four other Ivans. What are the odds of another Ivan playing in the same football pool as me and winning? Well, I should consider myself lucky that I wasn't able to spend the money that wasn't mine right? Ugh.

I had the really bad luck of succumbing to the disease of addiction and the really good luck of overcoming it, and I became a better person because of it. I'm not embarrassed about what I've done or where I come from. I wear my addiction proudly on my sleeve. It has made me who I am today and has given me an appreciation of life I don't think I would have experienced without addiction.

I'm not very religious, but I do consider myself a spiritual person. I thank my God every day for all that I have. I say it that way because there are many versions of God and I cannot accept the fact that any one religion is the right one, because that would mean all the others are wrong. I feel that God is to each person however that individual sees him, regardless whether he calls him God, Jesus, Allah, Krishna or anything else.

I take my inspirations wherever I can get them and came across this quote from the Bible. It jumped up and spoke to me in no uncertain terms of how lucky I am. How blessed to be given the gift of recovery and to be able to share my story, that it might offer help, understanding or inspiration to someone in need. I don't know if I interpreted this verse correctly and I don't want to know. I believe its purpose lies not in its ability to be interpreted correctly, but by meaning whatever it needs to mean by anyone who needs it.

> *"If ye then, being evil, know how to give good gifts unto your children, how much more shall your Father who is in heaven give good things to them that ask him?"*
> —Matthew 7:11

To me it means knowing all that I have done wrong, how much more can I appreciate what is given to me? It's about doing the next right thing and watching the magic that follows, and finally, how can I share that knowledge to help others? Well, I wrote a book.

Getting back to my really good-bad luck...in the early '90s, The Village of Freeport had applied for a federal grant. It was part of a revitalize Main Street program to combat the business closures in downtown areas. So many mom-and-pop stores in the '80s and '90s had fallen victim to the expansions of large corporations such as The Home Depot, Walmart, CVS, Target, and Olive Garden. Two years after I bought the Texas Ranger, The Village got the grant and with financial help from the federal government, funded a major revitalization project on the Nautical Mile.

They raised the streets and fixed the drains, which solved the flooding problem. They turned the crumbling concrete sidewalk into a beautiful 12-wide brick walkway with park benches and old-fashioned lighting. We got an esplanade and scenic pier and they buried the power lines. The Village's investment paid off and attracted many new businesses, which caused the stores that were run down to either shut down or renovate. The revitalization project brought more and more people to the Nautical Mile and business was booming.

This began the most profitable years of my life. In 1998, Rich and I bought a second restaurant, the Smithville Café, in Bellmore, where I had gotten my first restaurant job while in high school. As the Nautical Mile flourished, we sold the Smithville Café and picked up the foodservice contract on one of the two gambling boats that came to the Nautical Mile, feeding 400-500 people a day. We catered dinner for NY Jets every Tuesday night during football season. Real estate values were on the rise and I started building investment homes in Florida. By 2006 I was at the top of my game. Amanda was two years old and things were really going well—too well, I guess. It was the perfect time for me to self-sabotage and throw it all away on an insatiable need for a three-inch-long glass pipe. Maybe I felt invincible; I don't know what my original line of thinking was. But it was around this time that I started smoking crack on a regular basis. Two or three days a week at first, trying to hold back my irresistible desire for more, I was still able to hide my addiction from my family and friends. Five, six and seven days a week happened in flash, and I was now a full blown junkie.

Ivan Sayles

Chapter Thirty-six

CPCS 7

Criminal Possession of a Controlled
Substance in the Seventh Degree:
Arrest Number Five

Janice had moved out and I had been living alone in Seaford for several months. I was intermittently entertaining my crack friends whenever I was on a tear, while trying to maintain the façade of someone in recovery. My white middle-class neighbors were already sick of me from the domestic issues I had with Janice. There was no way in hell they were putting up with screaming crack whores on the quiet streets of Seaford Harbor at 3 a.m.

It was no surprise that the cops were watching my house. On one particular evening, I was getting high with a few people. The police waited outside patiently, knowing that eventually we would run out of drugs and need more. When we did, I made a call and arranged to pick up an eight-ball, which is three and a half grams worth of coke. One of the girls, Michelle, and I decided to take the ride and borrowed my friend Pat's car. I put a small scale in my pocket to make sure the deal was on the up and up and off we went, oblivious to anything going on outside my home.

We met the dealer, but he was short and only had one gram of crack. I bought it. We headed home, stopping at a gas station to buy new glass pipes and screens, and as long as we were out, I figured I would grab dinner: Snickers and a Gatorade. We took a few hits, then Michelle drove back to my house.

As we pulled away from the stop sign at the corner of my block, I was just finishing my dinner and all hell broke loose. Suddenly there were flashing lights in front of and behind us. Four police cars surrounded us and lo and behold, guess who was among them? My two favorite undercover cops: Carl and his partner John, the pride of Nassau County.

I asked why we got pulled over and was told, "Because you rolled through a stop sign." Good enough to hold up in court as the reason for stopping our vehicle, I suppose, but really? Four undercover police cars staking out a stop sign? Immediately, they pulled us out of the car, separating us and questioning us about where we had gone.

I was brought to the rear of the vehicle while Michelle was questioned in the front. Meanwhile, a different set of cops started searching the car. One of them told me to spit the drugs out of my mouth. I opened wide to show him a mouthful of Snickers. After coming up short on finding anything from searching the car, the cops accused me of swallowing the drugs, which I adamantly denied, opening my mouth again to show him the chocolate still there.

While I was arguing with the cop over what I had swallowed, he began to frisk me and found the scale in my jacket pocket. No big deal, I thought, scales aren't illegal. But a scale with crack residue all over it? Damn, I should have wiped that thing off after I had used it.

Once he found the scale, he started yelling "Code 9, Code 9" or some shit and the cops started dancing around celebrating like they had found Jimmy Hoffa. I mean, it really wasn't brilliant police work, catching a couple of crackheads on their way home from a buy. But hey, a win is a win.

Dirty scale confiscated, I was handcuffed and put under guard behind the car, while they continued to question Michelle.

It was only a matter of time before they found the crack pipe and the remainder of the gram of crack in the front pocket of my jeans. As luck would have it, those cops were so excited that they found a scale that they never continued to search me and placed me in the back seat of a police car. They then issued Michelle a summons for failure to stop at a stop sign and arrested her, too.

All alone and unsupervised in the back of the police car, I figured this was the best opportunity to get rid of my stem and the rest of the crack. Next to me in the back seat of the police car was a duffle bag and it was all I could do to not put my stem and crack in it. But I decided to put it in the seat instead, so I tucked my shit into the crack in between the back and bottom seat cushions. Given that the police precinct was literally right around the corner from my house and the supervisor was told I was thoroughly searched, the cops never bothered to check the car when I got out and I was never charged with possession.

Once at the precinct, Michelle and I never saw each other again. I was questioned about my activities that evening, and told them we had gone to get gas. Carl and his partner were convinced I had eaten a rock of crack cocaine and decided to take me to the hospital. I don't know if they thought they could test me for drugs or were concerned for my safety, but they had a bigger plan and my swallowing coke was part of it.

Michelle, I found out later, was also questioned extensively and had been told by the cops that I had suffered a heart attack, likely from swallowing crack cocaine and needed to be rushed to the hospital. She was asked to sign a paper saying that she had driven me to buy crack, and that I had purchased crack and eaten it in the car. The police told her this would help the doctors' diagnosis and save my life. Way to go, Carl! Thank God, she didn't do it.

The two cops who brought me to the hospital were not among any of my six arresting officers. They were from some kind of special detail designated for guarding and transporting prisoners. I guess it is important to try to intimidate a prisoner into thinking he has no chance of escape and these guys were experts in convincing my 145-pound junkie ass I had no chance of escape. I bet two of the prerequisites of this detail were to be able to bench press at least 400 pounds and to wear t-shirts two sizes too small.

I spent the ride to Nassau County Medical Center listening to these two knuckle-draggers talking about how tough they were and how many guys they could "take on." They also told me a very interesting story of a guy they beat the shit out of, because he gave them trouble. If this was meant to be an intimidation tactic, it was wasted on me. I was a threat to no one. I was every bit of 145 pounds, compared to their 220, and 235, respectively, as they had so informed me earlier. I was handcuffed in the back seat of the cruiser, strung out and hadn't slept for days. Where the fuck was I going to go? Kudos to those guys for keeping their game faces on the whole time.

Once at the hospital, Tweedle Dee and Tweedle Dumb walked me into a special area in the emergency room, pushed me down into a chair and finally uncuffed me, as a nurse checked my vitals and took my blood pressure. She announced it was normal but that my heart rate was at 105. As a doctor came on the scene, the cops claimed my elevated heart rate was from the cocaine in my system and demanded bloodwork. The doctor suggested that it might be from the traumatic experience of being arrested, dragged into the hospital in handcuffs and tossed around like a ragdoll, but my escorts were having no part of the doctor's diagnosis.

After my initial intake, I was brought to a standard hospital cubicle containing some electronic monitoring equipment, a bed and a chair. While Tweedle Dee handcuffed my left arm to the right leg of the bed in such a way that it was it impossible to lie down or get comfortable, Tweedle Dumb went to get coffee or flex his muscles for the nurses and tell stories of how he used to wrestle alligators or some shit.

I began nodding off as Tweedle Dee continued glaring at me as if I were Hannibal Lecter who had just stolen the doctor's pen.

Just then the doctor came in and I was told that, in order to release me from the hospital, they would have to do blood work, which I refused. Although I didn't swallow any cocaine, I certainly had plenty in my system, so blood work was out of the question.

I was crashing pretty hard at that point and as I continued to nod off, Tweedle Dee decided that his next trick would be sleep deprivation. Every time I began to slump over, my guard would grab me by the shoulder, shake me, and tell me to sit the fuck up. "You're not going to sleep it off on a nice comfortable hospital bed on my watch," I was told.

What did I do to piss this guy off? It went on for about 45 minutes until the doctor came back to check on me. When asked how I was feeling, I told the doctor I was feeling faint and lightheaded, so he instructed me to lie down. I said "You know, Doc, I tried to lie down before but it's really awkward the way I'm handcuffed to the bed. Do you think you could ask the officer to adjust the handcuffs, so I can be more comfortable?" The doctor did and the douchebag not wanting to be presumed a douchebag by the doctor, kindly obliged and adjusted my cuffs. The last thing I remember before dozing off was looking up at the seething expression on the cop's face.

They woke me up in the wee hours of the morning to release me without any blood work. My police escorts placed me, handcuffed, into the back seat of the cruiser, where the three of us sat in silence for the ride back to the precinct. There I was "ROR'd" or released on my own recognizance, with an appearance ticket in hand for court the next day.

At court, I figured my case would be adjourned and I would be told to come back another day, but that was not to be. I was remanded on $5,000 bail and given a new court date. This made absolutely no sense to me, since I was arrested and released the night before and then showed up for court. But it was what it was, and I was off to Nassau County Jail again to await getting bailed out.

OVERCOOKED

Chapter Thirty-seven

Me, Jen and Governor Andrew Cuomo

As a past President of the Freeport Chamber, member of the Nassau County Council of Chambers of Commerce and current President of the Nautical Mile Merchants Association, I occasionally rub elbows with local politicians, including the governor of NY State, Andrew Cuomo.

In 2017, a friend of mine, Laura Curran, a local Democratic legislator from Baldwin, was running for the county executive seat against the mighty Nassau County Republican caucus. New York State may be well-known nationally as a liberal Democratic state, but that ain't so in my home county. This is deep Republican territory. Nonetheless, Laura won, becoming the first female county executive in Nassau County history. Perhaps this was aided by her Republican predecessor, Ed Mangano, as he was arrested while in office and later convicted for taking bribes and conspiracy to obstruct justice. I'm very proud of Laura for accomplishing what she did.

I ran into Laura at a local event and she asked if I would be attending a $500-a-plate fundraiser hosted by Governor Cuomo at the Crest Hollow Country Club, one of Long Island's premier catering halls. The Executive Chef, Chis Palmer, used to sling

OVERCOOKED

burgers down at Jones Beach with Rich, Eddie and me. I can't wait for the "Ruler" to write his own book so you can hear his stories. I told Laura, "A thousand bucks so Jen and I could see you is a little steep for me." She said, "Don't worry, just give what you can. I'd love you there for support."

Cool. So, the day came for the fundraiser. I went to Jen's to pick her up and she wasn't ready; honestly, I have no idea what she was doing. No man does, but I should have been wise enough to tell her we were leaving 15 minutes before I wanted to leave and that would have solved that. We ended up being late and it was entirely Jen's fault. Sorry, Jen—my book, my story. The horror of this scenario has been played out by every couple across the globe, so I need not get into the details of our bickering on the 10-minute ride from our house up the 135 to The Crest Hollow.

When we walked in we saw a small registration table to the right, where I informed the volunteer that Jen and I were here for the "governor's thing." I was quickly informed that the governor was speaking and we could not go in the door behind her, as that's where he was standing. My sigh, which I'm sure was heard on the second floor, was enough for this nice young lady to wrangle an escort who walked us around to another entrance. Hmmmm, weren't we special?

We walked into a room of about 60 guests, immediately caught Laura's eye and went over to say hello. The governor was nearby, speaking to a few guests. I said to Jen, "Let's go get our picture with the governor." Jen was a little hesitant but I insisted, saying, "We didn't drive 10 miles all the way up the 135 to not get our picture with the governor."

With that, I gently forced my way from one end of the room to the other, through the crowd and right up to the governor. When he paused for a breath, I said ever so subtlety at the top of my lungs, "Excuse me, Governor, can I get a picture of you with my wife and me?" As he acknowledged me, I turned around and handed the guy behind me my cell phone to take our pic.

My mission accomplished, we hooked up with some friends of ours, Ben and Jen. They were also friendly with Laura but too hard-core Republican to have been caught dead in a scandalous pic with our ultra-liberal democratic Governor for fear their skin might have melted off from such an atrocity. I personally think they have Trump underwear and possibly MAGA tattoos.

Politics aside, the four of us went out for a very neutral carnivorous feast at Rothmann's. After some conversation and discussion over dinner, I was beginning to realize that perhaps we had been in the wrong room at the Crest Hollow. We ran into more people who had been at the fundraiser and one of the gentlemen, a Freeport Village Trustee by the name of Jorge Martinez, commented that he didn't see me at the event.

I questioned him, saying I was surprised the parking lot had been so full and the room was so small. Jorge said, "Wait, I was up in the main hall with about 400 supporters. Where were you?" When I told him the small room on the right by the entrance, he slapped his hands together and said, "Ivan, that was a private meet and greet with the Governor! It cost $5,000 a person to be in that room!"

"Oh, shit!" I said. "I must have pushed $120,000 worth of Long Island's snobbiest out of my way to get that pic!"

OVERCOOKED

Chapter Thirty-eight

My Three Moms and Paul Goldstein

Paul Goldstein and I were born in December of 1965, on the same day, at the same time, in the same hospital, to the same mother. She named me Paul David Goldstein, a name I never knew existed until I was 49 years old, when my third mom passed away. We were going through her things and found the papers from my adoption. I'll never know the life I would have had as him, because I was given up by a troubled 18-year-old girl, fearful of what her family and friends would think if they knew of her pregnancy.

She had told her family she was going to college, but instead went to a home for unwed mothers to ride out their pregnancies in secret. Her family eventually found out after trying to visit her at the school she didn't go to. She refused to let anyone come visit her at the home—until she was in labor and did not want to be alone, so she called her sister Harriet to be with her.

I spent the first few days of my life with my mother Yolanda (Landee), until I was moved into a foster home for three months, a holding center really, for children awaiting adoption. I would not see my mother again, save for a brief encounter 38 years later and would not come to know of her sisters or my cousins for another 11 years, when at the same time, I unfortunately learned of my mother's passing.

Three months after I was born, I was adopted by my second mom, Ruby, and her husband, Sol, my father. They named me Ivan after my dad's father, Isadore, who I recently learned was a pioneer in the Jewish deli business during the 1930s. Recently my cousin Ivy, also named after Isadore, showed me a book called, Pastrami on Rye by Ted Merwin, featuring a segment that my grandfather wrote for the Mogen David Delicatessen Magazine. Quoting some of his hard-and-fast rules for delicatessen owners:

- Avoid "knocking" a competitor's products.
- Maintain a neat appearance.
- Refrain from shouting at a clerk or sweeping the floors while customers are present.
- Open your store on time in the morning.
- Make periodic window display changes.
- It is essential that deli owners distinguish their products from ordinary groceries…and that they be viewed as delicacies.

Common business sense today, but revolutionary during the Great Depression.

Some expectant parents opt not to reveal the gender of their child until it's born. My parents decided to do the same and not tell my family whether they were adopting a boy or a girl, so I was aptly referred to by my family as "Cousin It" until I was ready for pickup three months after I was born. They brought me home and moved me into my new digs in Far Rockaway, NY. A few miles away and right in line with the runways of one of the world busiest airports, John F Kennedy International. I can still remember the planes flying over the building so low I could see the faces of the passengers in the windows…or I remember my mother telling me, figuratively, that you could see faces. I'm not really sure. Either way, it was a noisy place to live.

Shortly after the arrival of my sister Eve, it was time to move out to the sticks. We left the city and headed to the burbs on Long Island. It was considered the boondocks back then, and justifiably so, as there were still some small farms in town and access into our neighborhood was over an unpaved dirt road. It was there in Bellmore, Long Island, that I grew up with my sister Eve, and my parents until…

…the summer of 1976 when in July, our mother, Ruby, was diagnosed with ovarian cancer. I had no idea she was sick until I got home from camp. My father kept reassuring us that she was going to get better but on September 16, 1975, as I was beginning the 5th grade, my mom, Ruby, passed away. She was 35.

Three years later, our father married Myrna. She and her three kids moved in with us. I can't say we instantly got along, but it was not long before we all accepted each other and became a new family—we five kids and "The Parents," as we called them. We formed childhood bonds as all brothers and sisters do, that still exist to this day. If there is anything this life has taught me, it is that you don't need to be related by blood to be family.

Eve hired a private detective to find her birth mom and in 2000, she did. Mother and daughter, Joanne and Eve, were reunited. They bonded and have a great relationship and I recently had the pleasure of meeting Eve's mom Joanne at Eve's 50th birthday party. I decided to follow suit and in 2003 located my birth mother, Landee. My adoptive father was still alive at the time and I told him about Landee. He was happy for me and said he wanted to meet her and thank her having me, but unfortunately he passed a few months later and they never met.

Landee and I spoke on the phone a few times and agreed to meet. I made arrangements to fly down to Florida to meet her and her husband, Richard. Right from the get-go we were like oil and water. I guess things were never meant to be, between my mother and me. Maybe her guilt for not raising me herself was too much for her. Maybe my expectations were too high. Now that I look back, I suppose it was a combination of both.

Richard met me at the Miami airport in the baggage claim area. The plan was that I was to rent a car and follow him to their house and meet my mom. We exchanged pleasantries, and then we walked to the car rental counter. Making small talk, Richard asked me what kind of car I rented and what color it was. I told him a Ford Taurus and that I didn't care what color it was, as long as it wasn't purple. Richard said, "Oh, well, I have a purple Corvette outside that you'll be following me in." Open mouth and insert foot. Who the hell has a purple Corvette anyway?

I followed the purple Vette to their condo. The best way I can describe our meeting was "uneventful." I think I expected to hear angels singing or something; I really don't remember much about what should have been one of the biggest events of my life. We made some small talk and I was given a present, a nice thick gold chain that I had absolutely no desire for.

I remember being really pissed off, thinking, I didn't come down here to be bought off.

In retrospect and after learning more about who my mother was, I'm sure she was nervous and had no idea how to try and make up for the past 38 years. I found out during my visit that I was an only child and vaguely remember some talk about her having a sister or two that she didn't speak to. I asked about my birth father and was told, "I'm not ready to talk about that yet." Unfortunately, whatever information she had about my father died with her on May 24, 2012. After our initial meeting, we spoke on the phone a few times but we had less and less to talk about as time went by, and eventually the phone calls stopped. I never saw her again.

Every year on my birthday, I'd think about calling her but didn't. I couldn't understand until recently why we didn't hit it off. Now, years later, after speaking with my family and learning about her, I'm thinking it was just too much to process too quickly...for both of us. Perhaps we were just too similar in too many ways. One of my big regrets in life was that I never got to tell her about her granddaughter, Amanda, who was seven when Landee died.

I'm pretty active on Facebook and one day in January of 2016 while playing around, I saw a tab in Messenger that said, "Show filtered messages." I clicked on it and up popped a two-year-old message I hadn't seen before.

> Hi, Ivan! I have been wanting to reach out to you. My name is Gail and your mother, Landy, was my cousin. I only learned of you about two years ago. It explained so much to me. Landy was my older cousin and I adored her. She was witty and funny. That was growing up, and then she changed.... I am very close with your Aunt Harriet and have a good relationship with your Aunt Linda. You have some awesome first cousins, five actually. They have seven children and one on the way. I am aware you met your mom once and sadly, I guess it did not go well. I can only hope you know how difficult it was for her and how she carried this inside, her whole life. Perhaps she was a loner too long and just did not know how to respond.... Please know there is a family with open arms that would love nothing more than to embrace you. I really hope to hear from you.
>
> Fondly,
> Gail

In my response, I questioned Gail about why she referred to my mother in the past tense and she confirmed my fear, that my mom had passed. Wow! This hit me like a sledgehammer. Still, when I read Gail's letter today, the tears begin to well in my eyes. At the same moment I learned of my mother's passing, I also found out that I had a whole family who wanted to meet and get to know me! I thought my mother mentioned a sister or two, but this? This was incredible news. Talk about emotional overload.

OVERCOOKED

I met Gail and her husband at Rachel's and began having phone conversations with Aunt Harriet. She told me how secret her sister's pregnancy had been and that she was the only one of my mother's family and friends to actually see me after I was born. It wasn't long before I booked a flight to Florida with Amanda to see my Aunt Harriet. We met in Disney—neutral territory, not taking any chances this time. That morning, I called Harriet from the airport as we were boarding the plane, and she said to me, "I can't wait to meet you!" Excitedly I replied, "No, Harriet, to see each other again."

Amanda and I met Aunt Harriet and Uncle Jeff in February of 2016. The four of us hit it off instantly. There are some things you feel in your soul. Like when Amanda was born and Veronica kept screaming at me, "Is she OK? Is she OK?" and I knew beyond a shadow of a doubt, that she was perfect. I got that same feeling about Harriet, that feeling in my soul that everything about this was perfect.

The next morning she and I were next to each other in the breakfast buffet line and each got a bowl of oatmeal, both bypassing the brown sugar, raisins and toppings. When we sat down at the table, Harriet said, "Can you pass the salt?" and she began to generously shake it over her oatmeal. I was beside myself. The only other person I had ever known to salt their oatmeal was me. As silly as it sounds, right then and there, at that very moment, I knew I was home.

First Jen and Zoie met Harriet, then I met Harriet's kids, then they met my sister Eve, then I met Aunt Linda. Over the next year, our families merged into one. Eve, her husband, Rob, his daughter Hope, my nephew Eddie and niece Rachel (namesake of Rachel's Waterside Grill) live about 45 minutes away from Harriet and her son Chad and his family. They've established their own independent relationship—so much so, that when Eve sent me a picture of them all visiting Harriet without me, I had to tell my sister to, "Go find your own new family and leave mine alone."

Today we are one giant, happy family culminating when Harriet and Uncle Jeff came to my cousin Marcie's wedding in NY. She met my whole family, who greeted her with open arms; hugs and kisses were everywhere. I was especially happy that Harriet was able to meet my then-92-year-old Uncle Archie, the patriarch of our family. We ate, we danced, and we had a great time. Pride is the best way to describe how I felt that afternoon: pride in my family and the people who surround me. They are all wonderful, each and every one of them. I thank you for being there for me.

I think meeting Harriet was the final missing piece in the puzzle of my life, ultimately enabling me to flourish in a relationship, the first one I've ever had that was not tainted by drugs, and establish my own family with Amanda, Zoie and Jennifer.

That's all for now.

OVERCOOKED

Acknowledgements

Thank you to my friends and advisors without whose assistance OVERCOOKED could not have been produced.

Dan Austin

Linnea Boake

Bob and Libby Boitel

Megan Curley, the Guillotine

Morgan Dillon

Carrie Dolan

Lou Groia

Danielle Halloway

Roslyn Hart

Eddie Heslin

Lindsay Hooper

Mike Iannerelli

Sandy Kriegel

Darlene Lange

Heidi Newman, my editor

Ronie Purcell

Jimmy Rooney

Chad Schuk

Jason Shapiro

Nicole Tarangelo

Peter Weisz, my publisher

Special Thanks
The Sayles Family • Adam and Jessica Asch
Eddie Heslin • Richard Venticique
Without the love of this crew, I'm not sure I would be here today.

OVERCOOKED